Hickory, Dickory, Dock

Pantomime

orman Robbins

Samuel French - London
New York - Toronto - Hollywood

ISBN 0 573 06460 1

Please see page iv for further copyright information.

HICKORY DICKORY DOCK

CHARACTERS

Dame Foxtrot
Mary Foxtrot, her daughter
Willie Winkie, the Dame's beau
David, a gipsy boy
Baron Hickory, a real bad lot
Baroness Hickory
Herbert Hickory, their son
Slap
Tickle } the Baron's henchmen
The Wizard of Bong, an evil magician
The Sprite, his deadly opponent
The Black Imp, a nasty piece of work
Fairy Queen Snowdrift
King Neptune, ruler of the Enchanted Lake
Rose
Iris
Dewdrop } fairies
A Pixie

Chorus of **Townsfolk, Servants, Spirits of the Clock, Clockwork Soldiers, Golliwogs, Fairies, Water Spirits, Mermaids**
Junior Chorus of **Mice, Elves, Pixies, Spirits of the Clock, Water Spirits**

PRODUCTION NOTE

The huge Grandfather Clock that is the central pivot of this pantomine, is very simple in construction, and of necessity, quite light. Our original "Clock" was a kind of huge box-kite, with painted face and moveable hands. It had a large door at the front, and a black cloth back that could be moved aside to let the cast out unseen. Naturally we also had an opening in our backdrops to match, but there is no objection whatsoever to the Clock being placed at an angle to the wings of the stage, when characters either enter or exit through it. In Scene 5, however, it is better for the Imp to be in position when the scene opens. Small handles on the sides helped for lifting it. The sound of the Clock striking is, of course, done offstage.

In our original production, and several subsequent ones, the Fairies were played by men, which added a great deal to the fun, but women have also played them with success. Queen Snowdrift, is, as you will gather, played by a man, but to avoid giving away the surprise, was simply billed in the programmes "Snowdrift."

Music was chosen from popular songs of the day, and this must be left to the individual societies to select. The dialogue gives some obvious ones, but elementary surgery will allow almost anything to be used.

Keep the speed of the pantomime fairly rapid, and above all, enjoy yourselves.

Norman Robbins

For

ANN and ROY HUDD

and

JOHN BEDDING

ACT I

The Village Square

A typical pantomime village scene. Dame Foxtrot's cottage is up left

When the CURTAIN *rises, the villagers are making merry with song and dance*

SONG 1

At the end of the number they scatter to either side as Dame Foxtrot comes rushing out of her cottage furiously waving a large broom

Dame Shoo. Scat. Scram. Buzz off. Get out of it. You noisy set of what-nots. Go sing in front of your own houses for a change. (*To the audience*) Oooooh. I get this *every year*, you know. I should have a seduction in me rates. *Up* goes that curtain and straight away this lot start screeching their heads off. It goes right *through* you.

Villagers (*brightly*) Good morning, Dame Foxtrot.

Dame (*glowering at them*) I'll give you "Good morning, Dame Foxtrot" if you don't clear off. You've woken me up from me beauty sleep.

A Girl (*contritely*) Oh, we *are* sorry. (*She peers at her closely*) Still if it's any consolation, it doesn't look as though it were doing you any good.

The Villagers laugh

Dame (*scowling*) Oh. Is that so? (*Fiercely*) Well let me tell you, little miss Smarty-pants, that this face (*She touches her face*) is the kind of face men dream about at nights.

A Boy Well—I suppose that's better than seeing it in *daylight*.

The Villagers laugh as the Dame whirls round to face the Boy

Dame I *resemble* that remark, I may be just past the first flush of youth, but look at what happened the last time I entered the beauty competition. I got several offers, didn't I?

A Girl Yes. But they were all from Plastic Surgeons.

The Villagers laugh

Dame One more remark like that, cherub, and you're not going to be around for the next scene change. For your inflamation, me and the Venus de Milo are like twins. (*She strikes a pose*)

A Boy Yes. You're both very old, and not all there.

The Villagers laugh. Dame Foxtrot gives a bellow of rage and lashes out with the broom, knocking herself off her feet

The villagers exit laughing as she tries to sort herself out. Mary Foxtrot enters down right

Mary (*spotting her*) Mother? (*She hurries to her*) What happened?

Dame (*getting up wearily*) Oh, Mary. My little daughter Mary. (*Puts her arms around Mary's waist*) It's nothing, love. Just them village lads and lasses again.

Mary (*sympathetically*) Poor Mother. They *do* tease you, don't they?

Dame It's "poor mother" all right. That old skinflint Baron Hickory's after the rent money again, and he says if he doesn't get it *this* time, out we go. Lock, stock and barrel. (*Downcast*) Whatever are we going to do?

Mary We shall have to *pay* him, of course.

Dame (*startled*) Pay him? What with? We owe him *ten years' rent*.

Mary (*puzzled*) But Mother—what happened to the money we saved for a rainy day?

Dame Well—we had a very poor summer last year, didn't we?

Mary So it's all gone?

Dame (*nodding*) Every brass farthing. In fact we've got so little, I can't even afford to change the date on the calendar.

Mary Oh, *Mother*. (*She hugs her*) Still I suppose it *could* be worse, couldn't it? Come on. Cheer up. Things have *got* to start getting better soon. I can sense it in the air.

Dame Don't talk daft. That's the smell from the gasworks. Here—and talking about the gasworks—I've got the kettle on for a nice cup of tea. I'll just pop inside and see if there's any milk left in the cat's saucer.

Dame exits into the cottage

Mary (*sadly*) Poor Mother. She works *so* hard to keep up appearances. But I'm afraid things are starting to look black. If we don't get money from somewhere, I don't know *what's* going to happen to us.

Willie Winkie enters down left

Willie Hello, Mary.

Mary (*turning to see him*) Hello, Willie. (*She looks him up and down*) My, you *do* look smart this morning. Something special?

Willie (*shyly*) Well ... (*He squirms*)

Mary Don't be shy. You can tell *me*.

Willie (*embarrassed*) I'm going to propose.

Mary (*delightedly*) Oh, *Willie*. Mother *will* be pleased.

Willie I don't think she will. I'm not proposing to her.

Mary Oh? (*Puzzled*) Then—who's the lucky girl?

Willie (*squirming again*) It's you.

Mary (*laughing kindly*) Me? But Willie. I can't marry *you*.

Willie Why not? (*He laughs*) I bet it's never happened before. The Principal Girl marrying the local idiot.

Mary You're not an *idiot*.

Willie Yes I am.

Mary (*laughing*) You're *not*.

Willie (*insistently*) I *am*.

Mary is silent

Well don't just *stand* there. Tell me I'm *not*.

Mary (*bursting out laughing and wagging her finger at him*) You don't want to marry me *at all*, do you? Come on, now. Admit it.

Willie (*grinning*) No. You're right. Your mother's the only one for me, and I'd marry her tomorrow if it wasn't for one little thing.

Mary And what's that?

Willie Well, she won't tell me how old she is.

Mary I should think not indeed. No woman gives away secrets like that, you know. But I'll give you a tip. Try counting the candles on her next birthday cake.

Willie No fear. The last birthday party she had, there were so many candles on the cake, half the guests went home with suntans.

Mary (*laughing*) Willie.

Willie It's true. It looked like a forest fire.

Mary (*trying not to laugh*) She's not *that* old. As a matter of fact, I heard her telling our next door neighbour, only yesterday, that she'd *just* turned thirty.

Willie (*amazed*) Just turned *thirty*?

Mary That's right.

Willie (*scornfully*) Huh! It must have been a *U turn*.

Mary Now, Willie. Anyway, what does it matter *how* old she is? She's still a remarkable-looking woman. Do you know—when she was seventeen, the King of England gave her a *beauty prize*.

Willie Oh, come off it. William the Conqueror never bothered with all that silly stuff, did he?

Mary glowers at him

I'm sorry, Mary. I'm only pulling your leg. Me and your mother are going to get married as soon as we know that you've found a nice young man for yourself and you're ready to settle down.

Mary Oh—well I'm afraid you'll be in for quite a long wait, in that case. You see—I haven't met the right man yet, and until *he* comes along—I'll just have to stay single.

Willie But how will you know if he *is* the right man?

Mary Oh, I'll *know*.

SONG 2

After the song, Mary exits into the cottage

Willie (*to the audience*) Hey—isn't she a nice girl, eh? I could really fall for her. In fact I would do if it wasn't for her mother. Have you met her, yet? Have you? I thought you might have done. (*He laughs*) Funny old thing, isn't she? And that dress she wears. Did you notice it? She's had it for so many years it's been back in fashion five times. I asked her where she got it from and she told me it was the latest model from Paris. Latest model. It's more like a terrible *example*. (*He laughs*) Mind you—she's very intelligent. She's found a smashing way of getting rid of Peeping Toms. She doesn't draw the blinds. Still—I mustn't make fun of her, must I? After all, I *am* going to marry her. And that reminds me, I'd better have a little practice at me proposal, so will you excuse me a minute? I won't be long. (*He moves up centre and strikes a pose*) Gerty, my darling—Gerty, my sweet— Gerty, beloved—you've got big feet. (*Pause*) No—I'd better not say that. Ah— I've got it. (*He kneels*) My own little Gertitude. Make me the happiest of men—and marry somebody else. (*Pause*) No, I'd better not say *that*, either. (*He thinks*) I know—I'll shut me eyes and then I won't be able to see her face while I'm asking her. (*He closes his eyes*) My own little sherbert lollipop...

Herbert Hickory enters right and moves to Willie

Will you do me the honour of—er—er—er ...
Herbert What?
Willie Of being my own little—er—er ... You *know*.
Herbert No I don't.
Willie But you *must* do. We've been courting long enough.
Herbert Have we?
Willie Course we have. So how'd you like to marry me?
Herbert Not very much. You're not my type.
Willie (*opening his eyes*) Eh? *Herbert*. Herbert Hickory. (*He gets to his feet*) What are *you* doing here?
Herbert I'm getting proposed to. (*He laughs*)
Willie Huh, *you've* some hopes. The last time I saw a head like yours in this village, it had a *nosebag* on it.
Herbert Is that so? Well let me tell you, Willie Winkie, I happen to be a lot smarter than I look.
Willie Well that's *something* to be thankful for, I suppose. With a face like that you ought to join the Ku-Klux-Klan.
Herbert What for?
Willie You'd look better with a hood over it.
Herbert (*indignantly*) I'll have you know I've got a very sympathetic face.
Willie Well it's certainly got *my* sympathy.
Herbert Huh. *You've* some need to talk, Willie Winkie. My dad says they put better heads than yours on sledgehammers. *And* he knows why you're always wearing that stupid grin on your face.
Willie Oh, he does, does he? And why *am* I always wearing this stupid grin, then?
Herbert It's because you *are* stupid. (*He smirks and sticks his tongue out*)
Willie (*annoyed*) Oh, that's done it. Come here. (*He waves his fists*).
Herbert (*terrified*) Daddy—help.

Herbert scuttles off up left

Willie (*dashing after him*) Come back.

Willie exits up left. Slap enters down left Tickle enters down right

Slap (*imitating a trumpet*) Tant-a-ta-ta. Ta-ta-tan-tan-tan-tan-ta-ta-ta. Ta-ta-ta-ta-ta-taaaaaaaaa.

Tickle His Grasping Greediness, Baron Harchibald Hickory ...

They both turn to indicate Baron Hickory

Baron Hickory strides savagely in up centre

Baron (*snarling loudly*) Out of my way, dogs. Scum. Peasants. (*He looks round as he moves down*) Where *is* everybody?

Slap and Tickle shrug

How can I be expected to terrorize the entire village if there's nobody here? Bah. (*Lashes his leg with his whip in fury, and gives a yelp of pain*) Yeoowwww.

Slap and Tickle laugh

(*furiously*) Silence. Now then ... (*He looks around cautiously*) Do you two idiots know why I've brought you here today?

Slap and Tickle shake their heads

Then I'll *tell* you. It's because of something absolutely *terrible*. Dame Foxtrot's *clock*.

Slap Well, she *is* an old woman.

Tickle Everybody gets wrinkles at her age.

Baron (*cracking his whip with fury*) Fools. I'm talking about her *Grandfather's* clock.

Slap Oh, well—we haven't seen his, so we wouldn't know, would we, Tickle?

Tickle No idea, Slap.

Baron (*grabbing Slap's ear*) Listen, blockhead. I've just discovered that Dame Foxtrot owns a very valuable Grandfather clock. A clock like no other Grandfather clock in the world. It's absolutely *unique*. And I want it for my collection.

Tickle Well, why don't you ask her to sell it to you?

Baron (*outraged*) SELL me it? You must be *mad*. I've never paid for anything in my life and I'm certainly not going to start now. No. (*He throws Slap from him*) That old faggot owes me ten years' rent, so I'm going to throw her out into the street and confiscate *all* her furniture—including the *Clock*. (*He laughs evilly*) What do you think to *that* idea?

Slap Sounds all right—but what did you want *us* to come along with you for?

Baron To do the dirty work, of course. (*He indicates the cottage with his whip*) Into the street with her.

Tickle Here—now wait a minute. You don't expect us to throw her out on our own, do you? Not Dame Foxtrot.

Baron And why not, pray?

Slap Well the last time we tried to do it, she had a fit of historics.

Baron *Historics?* You mean *hysterics*, you fatheaded fool.

Tickle No he doesn't. He means historics. She told us what our ancestors were.

Baron Bah, you yellow livered cowards. I'll do it myself. Out of my way.

Slap Nobody's in it.

Baron Oh. Well. Yes.(*He marches over to the cottage door and knocks loudly*) Come out, you fleabitten old floormat.

The cottage door opens and Dame Foxtrot appears

Dame Oh, it's the River, himself.
Baron *River?*
Dame Yes. The biggest part of you's your *mouth.*
Baron Bah. I want my rent money.
Dame Thank goodness for that. I thought you wanted mine.
Baron (*roaring*) I *mean* yours, you decrepit looking lunatic. Either I get my money, or you get the shove. Understand?
Dame Well you'd better start shoving, Samson, because you'll get no money from me.
Baron Very well. (*To Slap and Tickle*) Throw her out.

Slap and Tickle dash into the cottage and bring out a chair. As they go back in, the Dame picks up the chair and hurries in after them. They exit with another chair and go back inside. The Dame rushes out, picks up the chair and rushes back inside with it. Slap comes out carrying the Dame, puts her down and goes back inside. The Dame picks up the Baron as Tickle comes out carrying Slap

Baron (*struggling*) Get off me, you old fool. Put me down.
Dame (*looking up*) Eeek, a gargoyle. (*She drops him*)

Mary enters from the cottage and Villagers enter L and R to observe

Mary (worried) What's happening? What's going on?
Dame We're being turned out. Convicted. It's a daylight moonlight.
Villagers Boo. (*They wave their fists at the Baron and his men*)
Baron (*snarling*) Silence, dogs. This old has-been owes me ten years' rent, and I want it.
Villagers (*loudly*) Boo. Shame. (*They crowd in on him*)
Baron (*cracking his whip*) Back. Back. Any more from you lot, and I'll turn *you* out as well. Now go on. Clear off.

The Villagers exit, jeering

Mary Oh, Baron Hickory. Won't you *just* give us a little more time?
Baron I'll give you five minutes, and if you don't cough up by then, you'll be out on your ears. (*He counts*) One-two-three-four-five. You're out.
Dame Here. They were quick minutes.
Baron I know. My watch is fast.
Dame (*wailing*) Oh. Turned out after all these years. Owwwww.

David, a young wanderer, enters up centre

David What's the matter, dear lady? Are you ill?
Baron (*snarling*) Who are you?
David My name is David, good sir. A traveller of the King's highway and owing allegiance to no man.
Baron (*prodding him with the whip*) Is that so? Well, I suggest you keep *on* travelling and don't poke your nose into things that don't concern you.
David (*annoyed*) I don't like your attitude, sir, and I like your face even less. Anything that causes distress to a member of the fair sex *is* my concern.

Baron Then I'll give you something to be concerned about. (*To Slap and Tickle*) Throw him into the duck pond.

Slap and Tickle grab David, laughing with glee. With a quick movement, he lifts his arms, then jabs his elbows into their respective stomachs. They stagger back groaning

David (*To the Baron*) Now if you'll excuse me? (*He turns to the Dame and Mary*)

Baron Not so fast, fancy pants. Do you know who I *am*?

David I've no idea but you're definitely the kind of man who'd make a perfect *stranger*.

Baron I am Baron Hickory of Dickory Dock Mansion and this old faggot owes me ten years' rent.

David (*to the Dame*) Is this true?

Dame (*sadly*) Yes. I have got a little behind.

Baron (*aside*) Not from where *I'm* standing, she hasn't.

Mary (*to David*) We're being turned out because we can't pay.

David (*smiling*) Don't worry. I'll see you're not turned out. (*To the Baron*) How much do these good people owe you?

Baron One hundred pounds, and not a penny less. (*He smirks*)

David (*astounded*) A hundred pounds? (*He recovers*) Very well. (*He takes out his purse*) Take this. I think you'll find the right amount in there. (*He tosses it scornfully to the Baron*)

Baron (*gloating as he grabs it*) A hundred pounds. Mine. All mine.

Slap What about the Grandfather clock?

Tickle Don't you want it now?

Dame Grandfather clock? He's not getting his greasy creepy-crawly measly mucky maulers on *my* Grandfather clock. I've had that ever since it was a wrist watch.

Baron Bah—keep your rotten old clock. *I've* got the rent money. (*He waves the purse*) Come on, you two. Back to Dickory Dock Mansion.

The Baron, Slap and Tickle exit up left

David (*watching them go*) Well, there goes my fortune.

Mary (*horrified*) You mean you gave away all your money, just to help *us*?

David Every penny of it. I never could resist a lady in distress.

Mary But we'll *never* be able to repay you.

David Never mind. Money isn't everything. It can't buy happiness.

Dame No, but at least you can be miserable in comfort.

David (*doffing his hat to them*) Well—good-bye. (*He moves away*)

Mary (*quickly*) Where are you going?

David Who knows? I'll just follow the road until it comes to an end, and hope to find my fortune waiting for me.

Dame You can stop and have a cup of tea before you go, can't you? I've got the kettle on.

The Dame hurries inside her cottage

David I mustn't stay too long.

Mary Why not? Don't you like it here?

David I think it's charming, but I have to press on to where fame and fortune will welcome me with open arms.

Mary Couldn't they welcome you *here*?

David (*looking into her eyes*) With you beside me—I think they *could.*

SONG 3

At the end of the song, David and Mary exit into the cottage as the inner CURTAINS *close.*

SCENE 2

A quiet street

The Wizard of Bong enters down left

Wizard So this is—(*he mentions the local district*)—and the last place on my list. The Magic Clock must be here *somewhere*. The Clock that holds the Black Imp a secret prisoner—trapped by the Fairy Queen—until the striking of the hour of one. (*He peers around*) But who can have it? And what is more important—do they suspect its secret?

The Sprite enters down right

Sprite (*brightly*) And what mischief are you up to now, dear Wizard?

Wizard (*startled*) The Sprite. Ten thousand curses. Can't you *ever* leave me alone?

Sprite Not if I can help it. It's my job to keep you out of trouble, so wherever you go, I won't be far behind.

Wizard (*annoyed*) Bah—well you won't stop me *this* time. When I lay my hands on that Clock I'll ... (*He realizes*) Oooops.

Sprite (*laughing merrily*) So *that's* it. You're after the Clock of Silas the Gnome. Well you're out of luck, my friend. It was accidentally sold over a hundred years ago, and has never been seen since. It completely vanished, taking the Black Imp with it. Trapped for ever.

Wizard (*grandly*) Not for ever. Only until the Clock strikes one, and then the Imp will be free again.

Sprite (*carelessly*) And what makes you think the Imp will still be inside the Clock? After all—a hundred years is a long time.

Wizard Because the Clock had *stopped* when the Fairy Queen imprisoned him, and only one key in the entire world can set it going again. The Key made by Silas the Gnome and now in *my* possession. (*He shows the Key*) All I have to do is wind up the Clock—and wait.

Sprite That's all very fine—but you still haven't explained why you're so anxious to free the Imp.

Wizard (*snarling*) Fool. It's because *he* can lead me into the Never-Never land and help me steal the Jewel of Miracles.

Sprite (*horrified*) You. In the Never-Never Land? You wouldn't *dare*.

Wizard Wouldn't I? Just you wait and see.

The Wizard laughs and exits left

Sprite (*distressed*) He's got to be stopped. If he finds the Magic Clock, there's
no knowing what will happen. Fairyland could be destroyed. I've got to
get help at once. (*Exits right*)

The Sprite exits right. Baron Hickory enters left

Baron (*muttering*) It's no use. It's no *use.* I've just *got* to have that Clock for
my collection. Now how can I get my hands on it? (*He thinks, with a fearful
frown on his face*)

Baroness (*off right*) Archibald.

Baron (*jumping*) Blast. It's the wife.

Baroness Hickory enters right, grim faced as ever

Baroness (*loudly*) So—*there* you are, Archibald. Hand it over at *once.*

Baron (*nervously*) Hand *what* over, my sweet?

Baroness The *money,* of course. Herbert tells me that Dame Foxtrot finally
paid up.

Baron (*scowling*) How *kind* of him. I must remember to give him something
for being so thoughtful. (*Aside*) A thick ear, for instance.

Baroness (*grandly*) Well? (*She holds out her hand*)

Baron (*handing over the bag with bad grace*) Here it is, my poppet. I *was* going
to give it to you as soon as I saw you. After all you know money means
nothing to me.

Baroness (*sniffing*) Only too well. Whenever *I* ask for any, I usually *get* nothing. I've never *known* anyone as miserly as you are. We must be the only
house in the village with a padlock on the *dustbin.*

Baron (*outraged*) Miserly? *Me?*

Baroness Yes, you. Why can't we have a new car, like all the other Society
people round here. Ours is so old the insurance policy covers theft, fire,
and Viking raids.

Baron (*snarling*) If you didn't spend so much on new dresses, we might be
able to *afford* a new car.

Baroness (*grandly*) I may spend a "certain amount" on clothing, Archibald,
but for your information—nothing *I* wear will ever go out of style.

Baron No. It'll look just as ridiculous, year after year.

Baroness (*annoyed*) Indeed? I shall remember that remark, Archibald. And
as soon as I return from the hairdresser, I'll have something to say. (*She
turns to leave*)

Baron Hairdresser? *Hairdresser?* Did you say you were going to see the Hairdresser?

Baroness I did. I feel it's about time I had a change of colour.

Baron Again? But Medusa—you've had your hair dyed so many different
shades, you're getting technicolored dandruff. You've got to stop spending,
before I go completely bankrupt.

Baroness (*snorting*) Bankrupt. Hah. Before we were married, you told me you
were well-off.

Baron (*sourly*) I *was*—but I didn't realize *how* well off. (*Groaning*) It's no wonder I've not been myself lately.

Baroness (*smiling sweetly*) Never mind, *darling*. Everyone's noticed the improvement.

The Baroness sweeps off right in triumph

The Baron glares after her with hatred

Baron Bah. That's really ruined my day. I'm so annoyed, I've a good mind to dash into Marks and Spencer's and shout "Woolworths". (*He looks around*) Where are those two idiots, Slap and Tickle?

Slap and Tickle enter left

Slap Here we are, Boss.

Tickle Do you want us?

Baron (*growling*) Not really—but you'll have to do till something better comes along. Now come closer and listen.

They move in to flank him

I've got to get that Clock from Dame Foxtrot. So tonight—when everyone's asleep—I want you to climb into her cottage through the bedroom window—and hand it down to me. Understand?

Slap (*puzzled*) What do you want the bedroom window for?

Baron (*hitting him over the head*) I *don't* want the bedroom window, you half-baked nincompoop. I want the *Clock*. (*Quieter*) Grab the Clock, lower it out of the window, and I'll be there waiting to carry it off to join the rest of my collection.

Tickle And what do we get out of it?

Slap Yes. We've been working for you nearly ten years, and we haven't had a penny wages yet.

Baron Why do you think you've been working for me nearly ten years?

Tickle Well, no money ...

Slap No Clock.

Baron Oh, very well. I'll give you your wages the minute we get it back to Dickory Dock Mansion. But remember—not one scratch on it—or *else*. (*He begins to move left*)

Slap Leave it to us, Boss. It'll be in your hands before you can say Jack Robinson.

The Baron exits left

(*Gleefully*) Did you hear that, Tickle? We're going to get paid at long last.

Tickle I'll believe it when I get it. The last time *he* took a pound note out of his pocket, the Queen blinked at the light.

Slap Yes, but this time it'll be different. Because if we don't get paid we'll tell Dame Foxtrot who's pinched her Clock, and he'll be up to his neck in hot water.

Tickle And so will I, if I don't get some money soon. I'll have to give up being a Juvenile Detergent and go back to inventing.

Slap Inventing? I didn't know you did any inventing.

Tickle Oh, yes. I've got a very mechanical mind.

Slap Yes, but it's too bad that most of the screws are loose. Anyway—what sort of things have you invented?

Tickle Well—I took the wheels of a Rolls-Royce, the engine of a Jaguar, and the body of a Cortina.

Slap The wheels of a Rolls-Royce, the engine of a Jaguar, and the body of a Cortina. All right. You took all these. And what did you get?

Tickle (*glumly*) Six months.

Slap chases Tickle off left, beating him with his hat. Dame Foxtrot and Willie Winkie enter right

Dame (*as she enters*) And another thing. I'm fed up with seeing that old Clock standing about the place. It doesn't work, so first thing tomorrow morning, you can get rid of it for me.

Willie (*eagerly*) I can chop it up for firewood and sell it, can't I? Here. I say, though. What shall I do with the works?

Dame Give 'em to Baron Hickory. I've been wanting to give him the works for a long time. Oh, and that reminds me. Speaking of time—don't you think it's about time we got married?

Willie Yes, I do—but who'd have us? And anyway—when *I* get married, I'm going to marry the most beautiful woman I can find.

Dame (*coyly*) I'm here.

Willie Oh, good. You can help me to look for her.

Dame (*warningly*) Watch it.

Willie I'm only kidding, Gerty. As a matter of fact, I was going to propose to you tonight after supper.

Dame (*pleased*) *Were* you? Oh, Willie. I knew this was going to be my lucky day. I'll tell you what. I'll do us a special celebration dinner, instead. Now—what will I get if I make you a meal like the one I did for your last birthday?

Willie My life insurance, I think. Can't we go *out* for a meal, Gerty?

Dame Go *out*? What for? There's nothing wrong with *my* cooking.

Willie Well, nothing a miracle couldn't change. Oh, I'm sorry, Gerty, but I can't face fish again. I've had so much lately, I'm starting to grow gills.

Dame But it's good for the brain, is fish. My first husband wouldn't eat anything else. He had fish for every meal. Bird's Eye made a fortune out of me.

Willie Bird's Eye fish for every meal?

Dame Frozen Cod for breakfast. Frozen Haddock for lunch. Frozen Plaice for tea, and Frozen Kippers for supper.

Willie And didn't he ever get fed up of it?

Dame He didn't have time. He died of frostbite.

Willie Anyway—I can't propose to you tonight, after all. I haven't any money to buy a ring with.

Dame Well, I'm not getting engagified without a ring, and that's final. How much will it cost?

Willie I don't know—but I'll tell you what. You lend me a pound, and I'll go out and get one.

Dame (*to the audience*) A *pound*. Can't you tell that this is a long time ago? You couldn't buy the wrapping paper now at that price. (*To Willie*) All right, spendthrift. I'll lend you a pound, but you'll have to give me an I.O.U.
Willie I.O.U.??
Dame I owe you one pound.
Willie (*pleased*) Do you? Well in that case I needn't borrow anything need I?
Dame (*to the audience*) There's one in every village, isn't there? (*To Willie*) Listen, Einstein. I.O.U. doesn't mean I.O.U. It means U.O. *me*. (*She gets a sheet of paper out*) Look ... write it down.
Willie (*producing a pencil*) All right. What do I put?
Dame I.O.U. one pound.
Willie (*writing*) You owe me, one pound.
Dame (*annoyed*) I don't. U.O. *me* one pound.
Willie (*baffled*) But that's what I've written.
Dame (*snatching the paper and pencil*) Come here. Let me do it. (*As she writes*) I.O.U. one pound. Right? (*She hands the paper back to him*)
Willie Right.
Dame Now I give you the money. (*She hands over a pound note*)
Willie And I give you the paper. (*He hands over the paper*)
Dame Then I sign it. (*She signs it*) And hold on to it until you pay me back. Get it?
Willie Simple. Well, I'll get off and buy the ring then. Ta-ta.

Willie exits right

Dame (*beaming*) Oh—I'm going to be bridalized at last. My trough is blighted and ... (*she stops suddenly, looks at the paper and reacts*) Eh? (*Furiously*) Willie—WILLIIIIIIIIE.

The Dame dashes off after Willie, waving the paper. The Wizard enters left

Wizard So—Dame Foxtrot has the Magic Clock, eh? Thank goodness I over-heard their conversation. (*He laughs*) Ha ha. 'Twill be easy to get it from *her*.

Herbert Hickory enters right

Herbert (*spotting the Wizard*) Oh. Hello.
Wizard (*aside*) H'mm. Maybe *he* can help me—without knowing it, of course. (*To Herbert*) Come here, lad. What's your name?
Herbert Herbert.
Wizard (*musing*) Yes—you *look* a right Herbert. (*With false joviality*) Tell me, Herbert, where do you *live*?
Herbert Here.
Wizard (*looking around*) Don't you find it a little draughty?
Herbert I mean here in the village. My dad's the Baron and my Mum's the Baroness. I'm their only child.
Wizard Indeed? Once bitten, twice shy, I suppose. Now tell me—where does Dame Foxtrot live?

Herbert (*smirking*) Everybody knows that. It's just down the road. (*He points left*)

Wizard Splendid. In that case, I'm sure you'd be only too willing to take me there, wouldn't you?

Herbert What will I get if I do?

Wizard You'll get a black eye if you *don't*.

Herbert Oh. Come on then.

Herbert escorts the Wizard off left, as Mary and David enter right

Mary —and this is Coronation Street.

David (*looking around*) Well, it certainly *is* a nice village. I think I'm going to like it here.

Mary I hope you do.

David Don't worry, Mary. Home is where the heart is, and mine is here with you.

SONG 4

As the song ends, the Sprite enters right

Mary (*surprised*) Look.

David (*startled*) A *fairy*.

Sprite No, not a fairy. Just a Sprite. But I need help desperately. There is an evil Wizard here in the village, searching for a Magic Grandfather Clock.

Mary (*amazed*) *Here?*

Sprite The Clock is under a spell placed there by the Fairy Queen herself. Long, long ago, Fairyland was menaced by a Black Imp who caused more trouble than all the Witches and Goblins put together. However, the Fairy Queen tricked him into hiding inside an old Grandfather Clock and managed to trap him with her strongest spell of all. Unfortunately, though, the Clock had been built by Silas the Gnome, a great friend of the Imp, and was made in such a way that when it chimed the hour of One, the spell would be broken and the Imp set free again. Luckily the Fairy Queen found out in time and managed to stop the Clock, taking away the key so that no-one could ever start it again. But somehow it's been stolen by the Wizard of Bong, and he means to free the Imp.

David But can't the Fairy Queen stop him?

Sprite Unfortunately, no. For over a hundred years ago, the Clock vanished from the old antique shop where it had been left for safekeeping, and has never been seen since. Until we can find it, we're helpless.

Mary What do you want *us* to do?

Sprite I'm sure the missing Clock is here—in *your* village, and I must get to it before the Wizard does. You can help by telling me the names of anyone here who owns a Grandfather Clock. Anyone at all.

Mary Well, Mother has one, to begin with—but there must be *hundreds* of them. The Baron has an entire collection.

Sprite Then I must find them *all* and pray that I'm in time.

The Sprite exits right

David Wait. Too late. She's gone. We've got to help her, Mary.
Mary But how?
David By looking for a Clock that hasn't worked for at least a hundred years.
Mary Then perhaps we'd better start with *ours*. So far as I know, it's never worked at *all*.
David (*eagerly*) Right. Come on, then. Back to *your* house.

David takes Mary's hand and they hurry off

The Lights fade

SCENE 3

Inside Dame Foxtrot's Cottage

A *typical panto cottage set. A table and two chairs are centre left. A large tablecloth conceals the false table top and plastic bucket beneath it. A huge canteen teapot is on the table, as are place settings for supper, and two small cups and saucers. One cup has a hole in its base and in the saucer, and is placed over a hole in the table which is over the bucket. An immense Grandfather Clock is left, fingers set at a few minutes to one. The inside of the Clock is stuffed with metal objects such as buckets, pans, dishes, and one or two brooms*

Dame Foxtrot and Willie are sitting at the table having supper

Dame Eeh, I *do* like fish and chips.
Willie (*unenthusiastically*) So I'd noticed. (*More brightly*) Here, I say. I nearly forgot to tell you. There was a fight in the fish and chip shop tonight.
Dame (*amazed*) Was there?
Willie Yes. Two fish got battered. (*He laughs*)
Dame Oh, get on with your supper.
Willie Here, Gerty. (*He looks round the table*) What's happened to the sauce bottle?
Dame It's in the place it's always in.
Willie Where's that?
Dame In the cupboard with my weekly payments cards.
Willie That's a funny place to keep it.
Dame No it isn't. It's *H.P.* sauce.
Willie Well can I go get it?
Dame You can if you want.

Willie exits right

(*Calling*) Do you want some more tea?
Willie (*off*) Yes.
Dame (*calling*) Yes, *what*?
Willie (*off*) Yes, I do.

The Dame glares off at him, then turning back to the table, picks up the teapot and pours tea into one of the cups. She goes on pouring as the scene continues.

Willie enters with a sauce bottle, shaking it vigorously

Willie Shake, shake the ketchup bottle. First none'll come and then a lottle. (*He sits at the table and pours sauce on to his plate*)
Dame Hey—where did you learn that?
Willie At the theatre last night.
Dame Oh, did you? (*Hurt*) You're always going to the theatre to goggle at them pretty girls.
Willie No, I'm *not*. Pretty girls mean *nothing* to me. It's *you* I love.
Dame (*brightening*) Is it? (*Eagerly*) Oh, Willie. Hurry up and finish your supper, then we can turn all the lights off and play Jockey's Knock.
Willie Jockey's Knock? What's *that*?
Dame It's just like Postman's Knock—but there's more horseplay to it.

There is a loud knocking at the door

Was that our bell? I wonder who that could be at this time of night? (*She hands the teapot to Willie*) Finish pouring the tea, will you. I'll go find out.

The Dame exits

Willie continues pouring into the same cup

Wizard (*off*) Aha. Dear Dame Foxtrot. May I come in?

The Dame enters backwards, followed by the Wizard

Well, well, well. What a pleasant surprise. (*He leers*)
Dame (*puzzled*) I'll say it is. Who *are* you?
Wizard (*beaming*) I? (*He laughs*) I am your husband's long lost brother.
Dame Long lost brother? (*She thinks*) Oh—I see. (*She gives a giggle*) Silly old thing, you. You're in the wrong pantomime. We're not doing Aladdin this year.
Wizard (*laughing falsely*) You will have your little *joke*.
Dame You leave Willie out of this. Now come on. Explain yourself. What do you mean, you're my late husband's long lost brother. Are you trying to incinerate that we two are relitations?
Wizard But of course. (*He indicates his face*) Can't you see the family resemblance?
Dame (*peering closely*) Eeeh. Now you come to mention it—you *do* look like my late husband—about ten years after they *buried* him.
Wizard (*roaring with laughter*) Ha ha. What a sense of humour. (*He eyes the Grandfather Clock*) That's a nice *Clock* you've got.
Dame (*touching her face*) Oh, do you think so? Well—yours isn't all that bad, if you look at it with your eyes shut.
Willie I say ...
Dame Shut up, Willie. (*She flutters her eyes at the Wizard*)
Wizard Is he your *son*?
Dame (*startled*) Him? Don't be daft. That's Willie Winkie.
Wizard Willie Winkie? Now haven't I read about him, somewhere? (*He thinks*) Ah, yes. I have it. He runs around the town in his nighty-gown, doesn't he?

Dame (*glaring at Willie, tight-lipped*) There. I said you'd be getting your name in the *News of the World*, didn't I?

Willie Do you ...

Dame (*interrupting him*) Shut up, Willie. (*To the Wizard*) Oh, he does talk. Now then. What can I do for you?

Wizard Well, now. I was wondering if you could manage to put me up for the night?

Dame (*blinking, then looking up at the ceiling*) Up where?

Wizard (*laughing*) Here in your cottage. You see, I've come a long way and all the hotels are full.

Dame (*shaking her head*) I'm sorry. I haven't a spare bed in the house.

Wizard (*producing a handful of gold coins*) I'll *pay* you, of course. (*He displays them*)

Dame (*her eyes popping*) —but if you don't mind squeezing in, I'm sure Willie'll let you have *his* bed for the night.

Willie I say ...

Wizard⎱Shut up, Willie.⎰*Speaking*
Dame ⎰   ⎱*together*

Dame (*to the Wizard*) I'll show you up to your room. Just be careful you don't bang your head on the cistern when you stand up in the morning.

The Dame leads the Wizard off right

Willie (*disgusted*) Well, I like *that*. (*To the audience*) Isn't that just typical? Nobody *ever* listens to *me*. (*He stops pouring*) I don't know now whether she wants a full cup or just half a one.

The Dame returns

Dame Right. You'll have to sleep on the floor tonight. Go get that old blanket from the dog kennel.

Willie Eh? I'm not sleeping on the dog's blanket. It wouldn't be hygienic.

Dame Oh, I don't suppose the dog'll notice. (*She begins to clear the table*)

Willie And where are *you* going to sleep?

Dame In bed, of course, where do you thi ... Oh—I've given my bed to that David, haven't I? Well, I'll just have to sleep down here as well. You'd better get two blankets.

Willie exits for the blankets

Oh, I'll leave all this till tomorrow. I'd better get into my nighty before Willie gets back. (*She does a comic "strip-tease" and gets into her night gown*)

Willie returns with two blankets

The Dame takes a giant mousetrap from behind the Clock and sets it. They wrap their blankets round them and sink to the floor a few feet apart

Willie Night-night, Gerty.

Dame Night-night.

Willie (*after a moment*) I say—Gerty. Do you know? It's twenty-five years tomorrow that we first met.

Dame (*sleepily*) Is it? I bet it rains.
Willie Do you remember?
Dame No.
Willie Of course you do. We went to have a meal in that buffet.
Dame (*wearily*) You mean "Buff*ey*" The "T" is silent.
Willie Not the way *I* drink it. Oh, come on, Gerty. You must remember.

SONG 5

As the song ends, the Lights dim and Willie and the Dame sink into sleep

Slap and Tickle, in full burglar kits, enter cautiously

Slap (*hissing*) Don't make a noise.
Tickle (*in a normal voice*) Pardon?
Slap (*loudly*) I said, don't make a noise.
Tickle Oh. Yes. I'll take my shoes off (*He throws his sack on to the floor with a crash*)
Slap (*terrified*) Shhhhhhh. (*He indicates the sleeping couple*)
Tickle Sorry. (*He slips off his shoes*) Where shall I put 'em?
Slap Oh—over there. By the wall.

Tickle tosses them over to the wall

(*Agonized*) Shhhhhh.
Tickle (*placating*) All right. All right. I know. Don't make a noi—— (*He puts his foot into the mousetrap*) OYYYYYYY!
Slap (*rushing to him and gagging him with his hand*) Shhhhhhh.
Tickle (*hopping around on one foot*) Mmmmmmmm—mmmmmmmmmmm. (*He wrenches off the mousetrap and gives it to Slap*)

Slap gets his fingers in the trap

Slap (*wailing*) Yaaaaaaaaaaah. (*He waves his arm wildly*)
Tickle Shhhhhhh. Shhhhhhh.

Slap tears the mousetrap off his fingers

Slap Come on. Let's get the Clock.
Tickle No, not yet. The Baron told us he wouldn't be here till ten.
Slap Well, how will we know that? The Clock isn't working.
Tickle Simple. I've brought an alarm clock. (*He gets it from under his coat and it goes off*)
Slap (*anguished*) Aaaaah. Stop it. Shhhhhhh.
Tickle (*horrified*) It's stuck.

They struggle with the clock, and at last it stops

Slap Quick. Let's get the clock now.
Tickle Wait. There's somebody coming. Hide.

Slap and Tickle hide behind the Clock

The Wizard enters

Wizard (*suspiciously*) I thought I heard movement. (*He listens*) No—all is quiet. Now to start the Clock. (*He produces his large key and winds up the clock which begins to tick*)

The Wizard laughs with triumph, and exits

Slap and Tickle emerge from hiding

Slap Who was that?

Tickle I don't know. But with a face like that, he should sue his parents for damages. Come on. Let's get out of here.

Slap (*startled*) Listen ... (*He looks at the Clock*) It's started ticking.

Tickle Perhaps it's going to explode?

Slap Don't talk wet. Clocks don't explode.

Tickle Oh, no? Well how is it that *time flies*?

Slap (*hitting him*) Take the pendulum out, dumbcluck. That'll stop it.

Tickle Oh, all right.

He opens the Clock door and all the pans, buckets, brooms, etc., fall out with a crash

Owwwwwww.

Slap Shhhhhhh. (*Annoyed*) What did you want to do *that* for?

Tickle (*hurt*) I didn't. They just fell out.

Slap Well, pile them all up over there (*He indicates*) and do it *quietly*.

Tickle piles all the things up quietly

Tickle I've done it. (*He trips over the pile with a crash*)

Slap (*annoyed*) Oh, stop messing about, will you, and get hold of this Clock.

Slap tips the Clock, and Tickle gets his fingers under it. There is a bump, off. Slap lets go of the Clock which falls back and traps Tickle's fingers

Hide. (*He dashes away left*)

Tickle (*howling*) My fingers. My fingers.

Slap (*turning to hiss*) What about 'em?

Tickle (*screaming*) They're under the Clock.

Slap (*hissing furiously*) Well, leave 'em, then, and we'll look for them later. *HIDE.*

Baron Hickory enters on tiptoe left

Baron (*furiously*) What are you playing about at? I've been waiting outside for ten minutes.

Slap (*indicating the Dame and Willie*) Shhhhhhhh.

Baron (*realizing*) Oh! (*He whispers*) Sorry. (*He sees Tickle and roars*) What's *he* think he's doing?

Tickle (*howling in agony*) My fiiiiingers.

Slap ⎫
      Shhhhhhhh. ⎧ *Speaking*
Baro ⎭   ⎩ *together*

They free him

Baron Now come on. Get this Clock out of here.
Mary (*off*) Mother. Mother.
Baron (*horrified*) It's the girl. Hide.

Slap and Tickle hide behind the Clock. The Baron gets inside it

Mary and David enter

Mary Mother . . . (*She sees the Dame and Willie*) Oh. They're both asleep.
David We'd better wake them, Mary.
Mary Yes. I suppose we should. (*She looks puzzled, then turns to look at the Clock*) David. The Clock. It's *ticking*.
David (*looking at it*) So it is. But I thought you said it didn't work?
Mary It *doesn't*. At least—it never *has done* before. (*Suddenly*) Oh, David, I'm frightened. (*She clings to him*) Something strange has been happening here. I *know* it has.
David (*holding her*) I'm sure there's a perfectly simple explanation, Mary. There's nothing to be frightened about. This probably isn't the Magic Clock at all—and besides, all the magic *I* want is here—with you.

They reprise the last verse of Song Four

Mary blows a kiss to the Dame as they exit

As soon as they go, Slap emerges from behind the Clock

Slap (*hissing*) Quick. They've gone.
Tickle (*emerging*) Right. (*He looks round*) Here, where's old bighead gone to?
Slap Oh, him, the fat old fool. He's skipped it and left us to carry the Clock
Baron (*emerging*) Oh, no he hasn't. The fat old fool's right behind you.

Slap and Tickle react

Now come on. Let's get this Clock out of here.

Slap and Tickle pick up the Clock and stagger off with it

Baron Hickory watches them vanish then begins to follow. Suddenly he stops, bends down and picks up a pin from the floor

A pin. (*He holds it up*) Now *there's* a good luck sign if ever I saw one. (*He laughs*) See a pin, pick it up, and all the day I'll have good luck. Well— this is *my* lucky day all right. (*He tosses the pin over his shoulder*)

The Dame and Willie wake, startled

Willie Eh? What? What?
Dame (*spotting the horrified Baron*) Eeeek. A burglar.

The Dame and Willie jump up shouting for help

Baron dashes off yelling as the Lights fade

SCENE 4

A Corridor in Dickory Dock Mansion

Dance routine with children as Mice and Servants with large mousetraps and/or cat

SCENE 5

The Hall of Dickory Dock Mansion

The Clock is centre, the hands almost at one. Slap and Tickle sit exhausted, one at each side of the Clock

Slap (*puffing*) Whew. What a weight.

Tickle I'll say. Still—we didn't scratch it, did we? Not even when we tripped up and landed on top of that big black cat with the white collar.

Slap That wasn't a big black cat with a white collar. It was the Vicar.

Baroness Hickory enters right

Baroness (*loudly*) What are you idle loafers doing in my Hall? (*She indicates the Clock*) And what's that horrible thing doing here?

Slap (*standing*) We've brought it for the Baron's collection.

Baroness (*outraged*) What? I'm not having *that* lying around *my* house. Take it away at once.

Tickle (*rising*) Not till we've been paid, Missis.

Slap We want what's coming to us.

Baroness (*outraged*) You'll *get* what's coming to you in a minute. Now remove that object before I do something drastic.

Slap Don't say she's going to sing to us.

Baroness (*outraged*) How dare you? (*Calling*) Herbert. Herbert.

Herbert enters right, in his nightgown

Herbert Did you call me, Mumsey?

Baroness Throw these horrible men into the street.

Herbert On my own?

Baroness Well, you don't think *I'm* going to help you, surely?

Tickle Nobody can help *him*. He's *past* helping.

Herbert (*drawing himself up*) Don't you talk to me like that, or ...

Slap } (*raising their fists*) What? { *speaking*
Tickle } { *together*

Herbert (*backing down*) I'll bleed all over you.

Baron Hickory enters right

Baron What's going on here? (*To Herbert*) Why aren't you in bed? It's nearly One in the morning.

Herbert These horrible men are upsetting Mumsey.

Slap (*indignantly*) We never laid a finger on the old battle-axe.

Baroness How dare you call me an old battle-axe before my son?

Tickle How was *he* expected to know your son wanted to call you it first?

Baroness Bah. Archibald—throw these vagabonds out *immediately*. Or else . . .

Baron Else what, my love?

Baroness Else I go home to Mother.

Slap (*to Tickle*) Looks like we're staying.

Baron (*quickly*) Oh, no you're not. If she goes back to her mother, she'll bring the old faggot back here, and I can't stand the sight of her.

Baroness (*grandly*) My mother is a very unusual woman, Archibald.

Baron I'll say she is. She's the only woman I know who reads the *obituary notices* to cheer herself up. And look at the way she carries on when she gets a slight cold. She moans and groans so loudly, you don't know whether to send for a doctor or a drama critic.

Baroness (*outraged*) That's *done* it. I'm leaving at once.

David and Mary enter right

David Oh, no you're not. No-one's going anywhere. (*To the Baron*) Just what do you think you're doing with that Clock?

Baron (*trying to hide it behind his back*) Clock? What Clock?

David That one. (*He points at it*)

Baron It's *mine*. Part of my collection.

Mary (*annoyed*) Oh, no it's not. We saw your men sneaking out of our house with it, and you following. You *stole* it.

Baroness Archibald! How *could* you?

David (*sternly*) You can just take it back to Dame Foxtrot's cottage, and the first thing tomorrow, we'll be reporting this to the police.

Baroness Oh, the scandal. What will they say in the—(*she names a local pub*)?

Mary (*kindly*) Don't worry, Baroness. If the Clock is returned at once, we'll forget the whole thing.

The Dame and Willie enter right. The Dame carries a shotgun

Dame Where is he? The money-grabbing, double-crossing, tight-fisted, bad-tempered old crab apple. I'll blast him into the middle of next week. (*She sees the Baron*) Ahaaaaaa. (*She raises the gun*)

Baron (*dropping to his knees*) Save me. I'm too beautiful to die.

Mary It's all right, Mother. We've got the Clock back.

Dame And I'll put *his* Clock back. Sneaking into my house like that, and tampering with me timepiece. (*To the Baron*) Stand up and be shot.

Baroness It was all a mistake. We don't want your dreadful old Clock. How could we put *that* in a place as beautiful as this? Think about the Old Masters hanging on the walls.

Willie *And* the old Mistresses bricked up behind them.

Baron Be reasonable. I'll give you anything. Just don't shoot me.

Mary (*taking her mother's arm*) Come along, Mother. It's almost one in the morning.

David (*startled*) One? (*He turns to look at the clock*) Quick! Just in case. Stop the Clock. Stop it.

Before anyone can move, the Clock strikes one. There is a great clap of thunder. The door of the Clock flies open and the Black Imp springs out

Imp (*wild with delight*) I'm free. I'm free. At long last I'm free.

Herbert That's nothing. *I'm* twenty-free.

Imp (*with a snarl*) You shall suffer for keeping me locked up all these years. I'll destroy your homes, turn your clothes to rags, curdle the milk, and blackout all the television sets in the village.

Dame (*in posh tones*) That was a party political broadcast on behalf of the Labour Party.

Imp (*with great menace*) Do you know who I am?

Willie Yes. You're a dirty little chimney-sweep.

Imp (*furiously*) No I'm *not*. I'm the Black Imp. Do you hear? The Black Imp.

Baroness Then you should have a bath.

Imp Don't you dare mock me.

Baroness Mock you? If you dirty my carpet—I'll *clock* you.

Imp (*outraged*) Don't mention clocks to me, or I'll turn you into a spotted toad.

Willie (*reacting*) Ahhhhhhh. He's done it. He's turned Herbert into a spotted toad.

All gape at Herbert, who looks uncomfortable

Baron (*snapping*) Don't be ridiculous. He hasn't done anything of the kind.

Dame (*staring at Herbert*) Do you mean he *always* looks like that?

Baroness Of course he does.

Dame (*to the Imp*) That's beaten you, hasn't it? You'd never be able to improve on *that*.

Slap Just a minute. Just a minute. You can't speak about our boss's son like that.

Tickle No. When *he* was born, folks came from miles around just to *look* at him.

Dame Yes. They didn't know what it was. The only time they should let *him* out on his own is Halloween. He might pass for normal then.

Baroness That's not true.

Willie Oh, you mean he doesn't?

Imp (*roaring*) Silence.

Dame (*to the Imp*) If you yell like that once more, mate, I'll tie a knot in your tongue and *swing on it*.

Imp Prepare to die. (*He raises his arms to cast a spell*)

David Wait. (*He steps forward*)

Imp (*glaring at him*) Who are *you*?

Herbert He's a gipsy. (*He pulls a face at David*)

Imp Nobody asked you, you little pipsqueak.

Herbert Oh, get him.

Imp (*to David*) What do you want?

David Well—to begin with—I'd like to know where you came from?

Imp Inside the Clock, of course. Where else?

David (*jeering*) I don't believe you. You couldn't get inside that Clock.

Imp What? You doubt my word?
David Yes. You're *much* too big to fit in there.
Imp (*angrily*) I'm not, I'm *not*. And I'll *prove* it to you. But after I have done, you will all *die*.

The Imp goes back into the Clock, and David quickly slams the door closed. There is a cry of rage from within

David There. That's got rid of him.
Mary But what if he escapes again?
David Don't worry. He can't escape till the Clock strikes one again, and that gives us plenty of time to find the Sprite.
Herbert Here—you can't leave him locked up in there. He might suffocate.
Willie I'll suffocate *you* in a minute.
Baroness Don't you speak to my son like that. If anyone's going to suffocate him, *I'll* do it.
Herbert (*pointing at Willie*) He's giving me *strange looks*.
Dame Don't be daft. You were born with 'em.
Baron I'm going to my room. I feel funny.
Dame In that case you'd better stay here. We need the laughs.
Baroness And as for you—now you've got what you came for, I'd be grateful if you'd take that dreadful object away as soon as possible.
Willie What a way to speak of her own son.
Baroness I mean the *Clock*.
Dame Oh, no. Not on your Nelly. I'm not having Liquorice Lenny bobbing in and out every time the Clock strikes one. You lot pinched it, and you can jolly well keep it. Come on, Willie.

The Dame and Willie exit

Baroness (*to the Baron*) Archibald. Take me to my room. I won't set foot in this Hall again until that thing is out of here. (*To Herbert*) Herbert—come with Mummy.

The Baroness and Herbert sweep out grandly

Baron (*to Slap and Tickle*) Oh, throw the thing in the moat.

The Baron exits

Slap He's got to be joking.
Tickle We wouldn't touch that Clock again, if we got paid *twice*.
David Leave it to *us*. We'll get rid of it for you.
Mary What are you going to do?
David Well, *I'll* go find the Sprite, if these two will stay with you to *guard* the Clock.
Slap *Guard* it?
David That's right. All you have to do is to make quite sure that nothing makes it strike again, and if anyone comes anywhere near it, just march them off to the police station.
Slap You mean—like a real policeman would?

David Of course. I want you to act just as though you were real policemen. (*To Mary*) I won't be too long, I hope.

David exits

Mary (*calling*) Good luck, David. (*To Slap and Tickle*) Well—I suppose we'd better sit down and wait.
Tickle No. *You* sit down and wait. *We're* going to stand guard.

Mary sits by the side of the Clock. Slap and Tickle go left and right to the wings, and get a policeman's helmet and truncheon each. They sing

SONG 6

During the song, Mary falls asleep

At the end of the song, Slap and Tickle march off in triumph, right. The Wizard enters left

Wizard Curses. The *girl* is still there. I must use *cunning*. (*He waves his hands in mystical fashion*) Hickory Dickory Dock. Mouse run up the Clock.

The Wizard exits to hide. A Mouse scurries in and performs a short dance before running to the Clock and trying to climb it.

The Clock strikes one, the door flies open, and the Black Imp emerges with a shout

The startled Mouse runs off

Imp Aha.
Mary (*waking with a start*) Oh. (*She jumps to her feet*) Help. (*She turns to run, but bumps into the Wizard*)

The Wizard enters

Wizard Not so fast, my pretty one. (*To the Imp*) Seize her.
Imp (*to the Wizard*) Who are you?
Wizard The one who freed you—now do as I say.

The Imp swiftly grabs hold of Mary

Mary (*struggling*) Help. Help.
Wizard It's no use calling for help. You're coming with us. Into the Never-Never Land.
Mary No. (*She fights to get free*)
Imp (*to the Wizard*) Aha. So *that's* why you set me free, is it? You're after the Jewel of Miracles. (*He laughs*) You stupid mortal. You haven't a hope of laying your hands on it. It lies at the bottom of the Enchanted Lake, guarded by King Neptune himself.
Wizard I *know* where it lies, my little Imp of darkness, and I know just how I'm going to get it. All *you* have to do is take us into the Never-Never Land.
Imp Very well. The entrance lies inside the Clock. Come.

With an evil laugh, he drags Mary towards the Clock. The Wizard follows in triumph as the Lights fade and the inner curtains close

Scene 6
SONG 7

On the way to bed

Choristers enter in pyjamas and nightgowns, holding candles. They dance or
sing, then exit

Scene 7

The village square

The Dame enters in outrageous costume, carrying a shopping bag with a
chicken's head and neck hanging from it

Dame Hello, Boys and Girls. Mums and Dads. Do you like the frock? (*She*
parades it) I got it from Oxfam. (*She sniffs suspiciously*) I think they must
have had an ox inside it, as well. Still—I got it for a ridiculous figure. (*To*
someone in the audience) What do you mean, "So we'd noticed"? Blooming
cheek. (*To the general audience again*) The woman in there told me it was
what's known as a "going-away dress". (*She examines it*) Now I've got it
on, I can see what she meant. The best part of it must have gone away on
its own. Still—it's bright, and you've got to have something bright these days
to cheer yourself up, haven't you? Well, *I* have. I've been so depressed just
lately. I had to go see the doctor about it. Well—he took *one* look at me,
and asked me if there were any other survivors. He examined me all over
and tut-tut-tutted, and I got all hot and bothered. I said to him, I said,
"Tell me, Doctor, how do I stand?" He looked me right in the eye and
said, "I've no idea. It's an absolute miracle." Anyway, he put me on a diet.
Bananas and Coconuts. *Bananas* and *Coconuts*. It hasn't taken any weight
off me, but I bet there's nobody *here* can climb a tree like I do. I've just
been shopping. In the supermarket. What a waste of time *they* are. You
do all your shopping in five minutes, and it takes you three-quarters of an
hour to pay for it. And the *traffic* when you get outside again. I spent half
an hour just trying to get across the road and nearly got knocked down
twice. In the finish, a policeman came up to me and said, "Here, you. Don't
you know there's a zebra crossing over there?" So I said, "Well I hope
it's having better luck than *I* am."

David enters

David (*breathlessly*) Dame Foxtrot. Come quickly. Mary's disappeared.
Dame (*startled*) Eh?
David I've searched everywhere, but there's no sign of her. She seems to have
vanished into thin air.
Dame But she can't have done. I've just been and bought a fresh tin of Kit-
E-Kat for the shepherd's pie tonight. It's her favourite meal. Where did
you leave her?
David She was guarding the Clock whilst I went to look for the Sprite, but
when I got back she'd gone.

Dame (*aghast*) Guarding the Clock? (*Reeling*) Ooooooooooh. she's been kidnapped by Sooty. (*Wails*) Owwwwwwwwwwww.

The Townsfolk rush in, alarmed

Townsfolk What is it? What's wrong? What's happened? Etc.
Dame (*distressed*) It's Mary, me little daughter. She's been abdicated by a
chimney sweep. (*She wails*)
David Don't worry, Dame Foxtrot. I'll find her.
Dame (*weakly*) Oh I'm going to faint. Get me some brandy.
David (*to a boy*) Water, quickly.
Dame (*firmly*) I said *brandy*.

The Boy dashes off

The Townsfolk fuss around the Dame

   The Boy comes back with a glass of brandy and hands it to the Dame

Dame (*knocking it back*) This is all your fault, David. Leaving her alone like
that. Oh—me poor daughter. (*She hands the glass to David and cries buckets-
ful*) Owwwwwwwwwwww.
David Oh, please ...

The Dame collapses into the arms of the Townsfolk with great drama

   Quick. More brandy.

   The Boy grabs the glass and rushes off. Willie enters in a panic

Willie What is it? What's happened?
Dame (*recovering*) It'll be ten times worse, now you've come.
Willie But what's wrong?
David It's Mary. She's been kidnapped by the Black Imp.
Willie (*awed*) Kidnapped? (*He draws a deep breath*) Well—there's only one
thing for it, then, isn't there? We'll have to go and rescue her—won't you?
David Of course—but I'll need help, Willie. How about you?
Willie Me? (*He is about to refuse, when he notices everyone is watching him*)
Oh—well—I—er—why not? I mean—if there's going to be any *trouble*—
I'll do my best.
Dame Yes, he'll do his best all right. One hundred yards in ten seconds, flat.
Willie Oh, don't be like that, Gerty. I can hold my head up straight with
the best of 'em.
Dame The only time you can hold your head up straight is when you've got
a stiff neck. Ohhhhhhh, me poor daughter. (*She does another dramatic faint,
but the Townsfolk miss catching her and she drops to the floor*)

   Enter the Baron and Baroness enter left

Baron What's going on? Why are you all standing here?
Willie Because there's no chairs.
Baron Bah.

   The Boy comes in with the glass of brandy

David Mary's been kidnapped, Baron.
Baroness Kidnapped?

The Dame gives a loud groan

(*Glaring at her*) And what's *she* doing down there?
Dame Getting up. (*She staggers to her feet*) Where's that brandy?

The boy gives her the glass

Baroness *Brandy?* Don't you realize, my good woman, that brandy is a slow poison?
Dame (*sipping*) I'm in no hurry.
David (*to the Baroness*) It's to steady her nerves.
Baroness Another glassful like that, and they'll be so steady she won't be able to *move*.
Baron Oh, pipe down. (*To David*) What do you mean by saying this old faggot's daughter has been carried off?
Dame Less of the old faggot, monkeyfeatures. (*She points at David*) He left her looking after that Clock while he went looking for a light, and that little horror came back and kidnapped her.
Baroness Leave Herbert out of this. He hasn't kidnapped anyone.
Willie Not *that* little horror. The other one.
Baron (*smirking*) Well, in that case—I suggest we banish him from the Village, here and now.
Dame Who? The Imp?
Baron No. The gipsy. (*He points at David*) He's the cause of this.
David (*protesting*) But it wasn't my fault. I was trying to save you all from the Imp.
Baroness A likely story. Banish him—before someone else is kidnapped.
Townsfolk Banish him. Boo. Clear off, etc.
David Wait ...
Baron (*raising his whip*) Clear off, you nasty little gipsy. We don't want your sort in our Village.
Dame (*loudly*) Just a minute. Just a minute.

All look at her

You lot keep your branmashers shut. It's *my* daughter who's been kidnapped when you've all finished. (*To David*) I've changed me mind, David. It wasn't your fault at all. It was his. (*She points at the Baron*)
Baron Mine?
Dame Yes. If you hadn't pinched the Clock in the first place, none of this would have happened.
Baron (*blustering*) It wasn't me. I didn't pinch it. It was Slap and Tickle.
Baroness Yes, it's all *their* fault.

Slap and Tickle enter

Willie (*spotting them*) Grab 'em.

The Townsfolk seize Slap and Tickle

Slap Help. Leggo.

Tickle What have we done? What have we done?

Willie I'll tell you what you've done. (*To the Dame*) What did they do?

Dame They set that Clock going when they pinched it.

Slap Oh, no we didn't.

Tickle It was going before we laid a finger on it. Some feller in a pointed hat and a nightgown wound it up. We saw him.

David The *Wizard*. The Wizard of Bong. He must have been inside your cottage.

Willie Oh no, he *wasn't*. The only ones in there last night were me and Gerty and Merlin.

Baron Merlin?

Dame My late husbands long washed brother. He popped in to meet me and pinched Willie's bed.

David (*urgently*) Where is he now?

Dame Still snoring his head off, I suppose. Go have a look, Willie.

Willie dashes into the cottage

David If it *was* the Wizard, we're all in *hot water*.

Willie returns in a hurry

Willie He's gone. The bed's not been slept in.

Dame I'll go get the soap and flannels.

Baron I don't like the sound of this. If I'd known the Wizard of Bong was mixed up in this, you wouldn't have seen *my* face around here.

Dame (*sighing*) Now he tells us.

David We've got to hurry. The Wizard is obviously in league with the Black Imp, and they've kidnapped Mary to stop her from warning us. We'd better form a search party.

Slap Oh, goody. I *love* parties.

Tickle Will there be jelly and custard?

Baron (*snarling*) Are you *part-* or *full-time* idiots?

Tickle Oh, full-time.

David (*to the Townsfolk*) Don't worry. We'll soon get Mary back again, and put an end to whatever the Wizard's plans are.

Willie But what about the Imp?

David We'll let the Sprite deal with *him*. Now come on, everyone. Cheer up. Give us a song to send us on our way, and we'll be back before you realize we're gone.

SONG 8

At the end of the song, the Townsfolk exit with waves and cries of "Good Luck" etc

David (*briskly*) Right. Let's get started. (*He begins to exit up right*)

Baron Just a minute. Just a minute. I sincerely hope you're not expecting *us* to help you?

Baroness Because if you are, you're in for a shock.

David (*stunned*) But—but you've got to help us.
Baron Oh, no we haven't. And neither have they. (*He indicates Slap and Tickle*) The only people *we* help are our friends ...
Baroness And for *them*—we'd go to the ends of the earth. (*She smirks*)
Dame I wish you would—and *stay there*. Come on, Willie.

The Sprite enters right

Sprite Wait. It's no use looking for them on this earth. They are in another world.
Dame What? (*She names a local district*)
Sprite No. They are in the Never- Never Land.
Dame That's what I said. (*She repeats the name*)
David Oh, do be quiet and let the Sprite speak.
Dame (*pushing Willie*) Shut up, Willie.
Sprite You must go to the Never-Never Land and ask the Fairies for help. They'll be only too pleased to give it, as the whole of Fantasyworld will be in danger if the Wizard gets the Jewel of Miracles. We shall all become his slaves.
David When can we start?
Sprite Right away. But first we must have the Clock, for that is the door to the Never-Never Land.
Dame Yes—and it's usually a door to door salesman who opens it.
David Quick. Let's get the Clock.
Baron Not so fast. That Clock is on my property. And no-one sets foot on my property without my permission.
Willie Eh?
Baron Of course—if *we* were allowed to come to this Never- Never Land with you ...
David (*surprised*) Well—of course you can. But I thought ...
Baron (*to Slap and Tickle*) Get the Clock.

Slap and Tickle hurry off

Baroness (*to the Baron*) Archibald. Have you gone mad?
Baron (*pulling her to one side and whispering*) Didn't you hear little Miss Tinsel-toes mention a Jewel of Miracles? Where there's *one* jewel—there's bound to be *more*, my dear. We could make ourselves a *fortune*.

The Baroness's face lights up

Dame (*to Willie*) I wonder what they're muttering about?
Willie I don't know, but I know it's a lie.
Dame How do you know that?
Willie His lips are moving.

Slap and Tickle stagger in with the Clock, which they place up centre

Baron (*hurrying up to them*) Where's Herbert?
Slap I dunno. He seems to have vanished.
Baron Hoo ... (*He coughs*) I mean—dear, dear.
Baroness Oh, my poor Herbert.

The door of the Clock opens and Herbert peers out

Herbert Hello. (*He smirks*)

Sprite Quickly. Out of the Clock, and I'll start the spell to take us into the Never-Never Land.

Herbert jumps out, and all fall back as the Sprite waves her wand

And now by magic fairy charms, the spirits I command. To come forth from the Magic Clock, and lead us to the Never-Never Land.

The Spirits of the Clock enter and perform an abridged version of the "Dance of the Hours". As the Spirits move downstage, the others enter the Clock and vanish, leaving the Sprite posed outside it as the dance continues

At the end of the dance—

the CURTAIN *falls*

ACT II

Scene 1

The Never-Never Land

Large toadstool houses in bright colours form the backdrop for this scene

Elves and Pixies dance holding garlands of flowers. A trumpet sounds, off, and they fall back as a parade of Clockwork Soldiers enter. The Soldiers perform a marchlike dance routine, then move aside as a line of Golliwogs enter doing a ragtime number. Following this, the whole chorus join together in a finale to the opening of the second half

After a pause for the applause, the Wizard and Imp enter down left dragging Mary behind, struggling to free herself

Wizard (*raising his arms and shouting fiercely to Chorus*) Begone.

The Chorus give cries of fright and quickly exit

(*laughing*) I'll soon show you who's Master here.

Mary (*struggling with the Imp*) Let me go. Let me *go*.

Wizard (*whirling to her*) Silence, you miserable little girl. There's no-one *here* to help you.

Mary (*looking round*) Where are we? Why have you brought me here?

Imp This is the Never-Never Land. Home of *All* magic, and hiding place of the fabulous Jewel of Miracles. The most powerful talisman in the entire world of Fantasy.

Wizard —Which *you*—dear Miss Foxtrot—are going to help me to steal.

Mary (*indignantly*) Oh, no I'm not. (*She fights to free herself again*)

Wizard (*snarling*) You have no choice. Within a few hours, your precious David will be here to try and rescue you, if that interfering Sprite does as I think she will. But I shall be ready for him. (*He laughs evilly*)

Mary What are you going to do?

Wizard Wait and *see*. (*Briskly*) In the meantime, the Imp will take you in one direction, whilst *I* go in the other. When David asks the Fairies for their help, they will follow the Imp, thus leaving the way to the Enchanted Lake unguarded, and giving me an open door to the Jewel of Miracles.

Mary (*firmly*) I won't go with him.

Imp (*grinning*) Oh, yes you *will*.

Wizard (*to the Imp*) One moment. We must arrange a meeting place.

The Imp releases Mary and goes to join him

(*to Mary*) It's no use trying to escape, my dear. Until my friend the Imp touches you again, you're unable to move. (*He rapidly throws a "spell" at her*) Enjoy your "rest".

31

The Wizard laughs, then moves upstage with the Imp. The Lights fade, leaving Mary in a spotlight

Mary (*struggling*) It's no use. I'm surrounded by an invisible wall. (*Sadly*) Oh, David, where are you? (*She sinks to the floor*)

SONG 9

At the end of the song, the Lights brighten again. The Wizard and Imp move apart as their conversation ends

Wizard So be it. I shall wait for you there.

The Wizard exits right

Imp (*grabbing hold of Mary*) Come along, my pretty one. You can move again, now.

Mary suddenly stamps hard on his foot

Owwwwwwwww.

Mary dashes off up left

(*Hopping after her*) Come back. Stop.

The Imp exits after Mary. The Sprite and David enter

Sprite They cannot be too far ahead, for the spell *I* used to carry us here was far more powerful than the Imp's. Still, I'll make sure he hasn't set a trap for us. Wait here.

The Sprite exits

David (*looking around*) So this is the Never-Never Land. I'd no idea it was so big. If it weren't for the Sprite's help, I don't think we'd stand a chance of finding Mary and rescuing her.

Mary hurries in up left

(*Surprised*) Mary.
Mary (*delighted*) Oh, David. (*She runs to him and embraces him*)
David (*delighted*) Thank goodness you're safe.

The Imp enters up left

Imp (*with an evil grin*) So—the love-birds are together again, eh? Then you shall *die* together.
David (*scornfully*) Huh. We're not scared of a little thing like *you*, even if you *have* got a face like a nightmare.
Imp (*annoyed*) I *haven't* got a face like a nightmare.
David Oh, yes you have. You could make a good living hiring yourself out to scare people with hiccups.
Imp (*furiously*) I couldn't. I couldn't. (*Snarling*) You'll pay for that. I'll turn you into a big yellow toad.
David (*laughing*) You couldn't turn a cow into a field.

Imp (*screeching*) Couldn't I? Well watch this. (*He raises his arms*).

The Sprite enters behind him

Sprite (*firmly*) Stop.
Imp (*turning in fury*) The Sprite.
Sprite Harm one hair of these good people's heads, and you shall suffer dearly for it.
Imp (*snarling*) By *who's* action? Haven't you forgotten that *I* am the Black Imp?
Sprite And haven't *you* forgotten that *I* am one of the Guardians of the Jewel of Miracles? (*She raises her wand*) Begone!

A beam of white light falls on the Imp. With a scream of pain, he staggers and doubles up in agony

Imp Stop. Stop. I'll leave them alone. I won't harm them.
Sprite Very well.

The Sprite waves her wand and the light goes out

Imp (*rising painfully*) You have the upper hand now, but just wait till the Wizard gets his hands on the Jewel. You will *all* suffer.

The Imp exits quickly

Sprite What he says is true. If the Jewel *does* fall into the Wizard's hands, it will be the end of everything. Nothing can equal the power of *that*.
Mary But where is it?
Sprite At the bottom of the Enchanted Lake, in the safekeeping of King Neptune and his Mermaid Court.
David Then how can the Wizard steal it?
Sprite I'm not sure, but Neptune is an old man, and the Wizard is extremely cunning. Our only hope is to get to the Mermaid Court first, and warn them of the danger.
Mary But how do we do that? We can't go to the bottom of the Lake. We wouldn't be able to breathe.
Sprite That's where the Fairy Queen will help. She will give you the power to live underwater as easily as you live on land. And not only that, with her to help us, we'll have nothing to fear from the Wizard.
David Then take us to see her right away. There's not a minute to lose.
Sprite Come. (*She flourishes her wand*) To the Court of the Fairy Queen.

The Sprite, David and Mary exit up right. The Dame and Willie enter down left. Dame is dressed as a Girl Guide, Willie as a Boy Scout in shorts

Dame Oh, look. Footsteps. (*She bends and picks up a shoe inner sole*)
Willie (*wide-eyed*) Here, Gerty. This must be where Rabbitson Creasote lived with Man Fried Egg.
Dame (*nervously clinging to him and looking around*) That means there might be *cannonballs* about. We could be *eaten* alive.
Willie Don't get in a stew, Gerty. *I'll* protect you.

Dame You? That's a laugh. You couldn't say boo to a goose, never mind, protect *me*.

Willie Oh no? Well what about the last time I stuck up for you, eh? I could have beaten that feller using only one hand.

Dame I know. And you might have done, if he hadn't hit you with his crutches.

Willie Well—I had him worried, didn't I?

Dame Yes. He thought he'd killed you. (*She gives a sudden shriek*) Oooooooooh.

Willie (*startled*) Whattisit? (*He spins round in panic*)

Dame (*pointing off*) There's something moving over there.

Willie (*terrified*) Help ...

The Dame and Willie cling to each other in fright, eyes tightly closed

A tiny Pixie enters and stands looking at them

Pixie (*tapping Willie, lightly*) Excuse me.

Willie Ahhhhhhh. (*He passes out in the Dame's arms*)

Dame (*opening her eyes and seeing the Pixie*) Oh—it's Ronnie Corbett.

Pixie Hello.

Dame (*pushing Willie to his feet again*) Hello.

Willie (*gazing at the Pixie*) Hey—it's a little *Pixie*. I wonder what he wants.

Dame Well, I hope he's not collecting for the National Elf Service, because I've left my purse at home.

Pixie Oh, no. I'm not collecting for anything. I just want to know if I can call all my friends to meet you?

Dame Call all your friends to meet us? Well, of course you can, can't he, Willie?

Willie Yes. Bring 'em in.

The Pixie signals off

Other Pixies enter to form a semi-circle round the Dame and Willie

Dame Well, aren't you pretty? Oh, I'd better introduce myself. I'm Dame Foxtrot, and this is Willie Winkie.

Pixie Oh, we know who you *are*. That's why we've come to see if you will help us.

Willie What do you want us to do?

Pixie We want you to sing a song for us. And as loudly as possible, please.

Dame You want us to sing a song for you, and as loudly as possible?

Pixie That's right. And then we'll take you to see the Fairy Queen.

Willie All right.

Dame (*preening*) They must have heard what wonderful voices we've got, Willie. (*To the Pixies*) That's why you want us to sing for you, isn't it?

Pixie Oh, no. *We* heard you both had *terrible* voices, and as there's a naughty old Wolf hiding over there in the trees, we thought if you sang very loudly, you'd frighten it away.

Dame (*taken aback*) Well, you saucy bits of beetroot. Just for that, we *will* sing something—and you can help us.

SONG 10

After the song, the Pixies lead Dame and Willie off right. Slap and Tickle enter left

Slap (*looking round*) Look at these funny houses.

Tickle I bet there's not Mush-room in 'em. (*He moves down centre*) So *this* is the Never-Never Land, is it? I wonder where the others have got to?

Slap They must be in front of us. I wonder if they've left a message. (*He looks around*) Ah. (*He picks up a square of white tissue paper*)

Tickle (*eagerly*) What's it say?

Slap Nothing. It's blank.

Tickle Fool. The writing's on the other side. (*He snatches it*) Oh—it's in some sort of code.

Slap (*looking*) Idiot. You've got it upside down. Give it here. (*He takes it back and reads*)

Tickle What's it say *now*?

Slap (*reading*) "Don't forget to wash your hands." (*He tosses it down*)

Tickle (*suddenly*) Oh—look. (*He points off left*) Something's coming through those bushes.

Slap (*gazing off left*) It's getting closer. I can hear its horrible shuddering breathing.

Tickle (*clutching Slap closely*) Ahhhhhhh. I can *see* it. Great staring eyes, pointed ears, a gaping red mouth and teeth like daggers.

Slap It's coming towards us.

They cower in fright

Herbert enters left

Herbert Hello. I thought I'd lost you.

Slap (*looking up*) Herbert.

Herbert Did you miss me?

Tickle Yes—with both guns. I must be out of practice.

Herbert It's no use trying to provoke me, 'cos I'm not going to lose my temper. *I've* got to be careful when I lose my temper in case somebody gets *hurt*.

Slap Huh. Who could get hurt when *you* lose your temper?

Herbert *Me.*

Slap That's true. I've seen better bodies than yours in a used car lot.

Herbert Huh, muscles aren't everything, you know. I've got *brains*.

Tickle Brains? You?

Herbert Yes, me. I know lots of things, I do. Did you know, for instance, that there are so many people in China, every time I breathe out, *four* of them die.

Slap (*sniffing*) I'm not surprised. You've been eating garlic again.

Herbert Ask me a question.

Tickle All right. What's hairy and coughs?

Herbert What's hairy and coughs? I don't know.

Tickle A coconut with bronchitis. (*He laughs*)

Herbert You're trying to turn me into a joke, aren't you?

Slap Of course we're not. You're a joke already.

Herbert (*put out*) Are you insinuating that I'm not all here?

Tickle Good heavens, no. We hope you *are* all here. It'd be awful if there were any more of you to come.

Herbert You think you're clever, don't you? Well, just remember. He who laughs last ...

Slap Generally misses the next joke.

Tickle And speaking of jokes ...

The Baroness enters on the Baron's back

Baroness (*alighting*) Ooooooch, Archibald. I'm so *saddlesore*. You don't make a very good horse.

Slap Try Herbert. He looks like a horse.

Herbert Do you *mind*?

Tickle *We* don't, but does your father?

Baron (*snarling*) Of course I don't. (*He realizes*) How *dare* you?

Baroness Say something to them, Archibald.

Slap and Tickle rear up

Baron (*weakly*) Hello.

Baroness (*angrily*) Not like that, you fool. Say something *nasty*.

Baron Castor Oil?

Baroness Bah, you're as bad as they are. Can't you stand up and defend your wife and child? Why, I believe you'd just *stand* there and watch them carry us off.

Baron (*indignantly*) I certainly *wouldn't*. I'd close my eyes.

Herbert (*suddenly stiffening*) Here—I've got a funny feeling. It's like eyes watching us.

Baron That's the audience, you fathead.

Baroness No. Herbert's right. *I've* got it too. It's like an icy cold trickle running down my spine.

Slap So *that's* where I put my Orange Maid.

The Black Imp appears behind them

Imp Aha.

Everyone turns to see him

Prepare to *die*. (*He laughs evilly*)

Baron Wait—wait. Don't kill us. We're on *your* side.

Imp *My* side?

Baroness Yes. We don't care about the girl. All we want is the money. The jewels.

Imp Jewels?

Baron Yes. Take us to where *they* are, and you can do what you want with her.

Imp (*to the audience*) And I thought *I* was the villain in this show. (*To the others, with a cry of rage*) No—you shall *all* die.

Slap All right, then. Kill us. Do what you want. (*He fights back a mock tear of heroism*) We're not afraid.

Tickle (*bravely*) Just give us one last request.

Imp (*suspiciously*) What is it?
Slap (*fighting back tears*) Give us just one minute to say our farewells.
Imp (*with bad grace*) Oh, very well. Get on with it.
Tickle (*sniffing*) I can't. Not with you watching me. You'll have to turn your
   back. (*He cries crocodile tears*)

With a scowl of disgust, the Imp turns his back

   At once, Slap, Tickle, the Baron and the Baroness dash off

Herbert remains, oblivious

Imp Time's up. (*He turns quickly with arms raised*) Abracad ... (*He realizes*)
   Where *are* they? Where did they go?
Herbert That way. (*He points*)
Imp Thank you. (*He dashes off after them, then reacts, turns and faces Herbert*)
   Grrrrrrrrr.
Herbert (*suddenly realizing*) Oo-er.

   *With a yelp of fright, Herbert dashes off left, pursued by the Imp, as the inner
   curtains close*

SCENE 2

A woodland path

                              As required

SCENE 3

The Fairy Glen
A woodland scene. The Throne of the Fairy Queen is centre, facing upstage.

*Huge gossamer wings emerge from the sides and top of the throne, and a tiara
sparkles atop a head of golden hair. It is obvious that Her Royal Majesty, the
Fairy Queen is sitting there. Her Fairy subjects are engaged in a dainty frolic
with garlands of flowers, below the throne. At the end of the dance, Rose and
Iris, two of the Fairies, move down centre, whilst the rest of the Fairies adopt
graceful poses around the stage*

Rose Ah, it's all very well, but since our Queen banished Iolanthe, fairy revels
   have not been what they were.
Iris Iolanthe was the life and soul of Fairyland. Why, she wrote all our songs
   and arranged all our dances. We sing her songs and we trip her measures,
   but we don't enjoy ourselves.
Rose To think that five-and-twenty years have elapsed since she was banished.
   What could she have done to deserve so terrible a punishment?
Iris She auditioned for Gilbert and Sullivan and got turned down.

Rose *Poor* Iolanthe.

Iris It upset our Queen *dreadfully*. In fact, I'm sure that's the reason she's been sitting on the Royal Throne all this time. Wondering if she ought to give her a second chance. *(She sighs)* Oh, if only we *knew* what she was thinking, it wouldn't be so bad; but there she sits, staring into space and never speaks a word.

Rose Perhaps ... *(She stops)*

Iris Yes?

Rose Perhaps she's feeling her age.

Iris Oh—I never thought of *that*. How old *is* she?

Queen *(firmly)* Don't you *dare*.

The Throne turns to face front, thus revealing Queen Snowdrift of the Fairies. She is very much the worse for wear, in a mis-shapen gown, dented tiara and clutching a wilted wand. Black elastic sided boots grace her feet, and when she stands, it can be seen that her wings are darned. The glorious gossamer ones, plus golden hair and tiara remain glued to the Throne

Rose⎫ *(curtsying low)* Your Majesty. ⎰ *Speaking*
Iris ⎭   ⎱ *together*

Queen *(moving down centre)* I'll give you, "Your Majesty", in a minute. How *dare* you ask about my age? My age is entirely my own business—and I've been in business for some time.

Iris I didn't mean to be rude, your Majesty.

Queen No, I'm sure you didn't. It was that one there, egging you on again. *(She indicates Rose)* Oh, I know all about her and her little tricks. Thinks she's going to take over when I retire. *(She sniffs)* Fat chance *she's* got. Not with a figure like hers.

Rose *(indignantly)* And what's wrong with my figure?

Queen *(amused)* What's *wrong* with it? What's *right* with it, you mean. You're so thin, every time you drink tomato juice, you look like a thermometer.

Rose *(stung)* Well that's better than being *overweight* like you. You're so fat, you're running out of places to hide it.

Queen That's a lie. *I* have a perfect figure. And thanks to my Tupperware corsets, it's going to *remain* that way.

Iris Tupperware *corsets*, your Majesty?

Queen That's right, Iris. I've worn them for years.

Iris And do they hold you in?

Queen No—but they keep what I've got fresh. *(She laughs archly)*

Dewdrop *(coming downstage, her legs pressed tightly together)* Excuth me.

Queen Snowdrift turns in surprise

Queen Pårdon?

Dewdrop *(shaking her head)* Excuth me.

Queen *(looking her up and down, then realizing)* Oh—yes—of course, Dewdrop. Off you go. And don't forget. Flush twice.

Dewdrop *(shaking her head)* No, no. I think thomething thtrange ith happening. Thome-one'th coming thith way.

Queen Thome-one? I mean—*someone*? Who?

Dewdrop It theems to be thtrangerth.
Queen Thtrangerth? (*To the Fairies*) Quickly, everyone. It's visiting time.

The Fairies scramble to their feet

Don't just stand there, Rose. Form an escort for them.
Rose Not till I get an apology.
Queen (*tiredly*) Oh—it's like being in management at Ford's. Don't you real-
ize that these will be the first visitors we've had in years? You've got to
help me impress them.
Rose Impress them? You couldn't even impress *me*.
Queen No—but I could dot you with me magic wand, and *that'd* make an
impression. Now get cracking.
Rose Oh, all right. But after they've gone, I'm calling everybody out on strike.

Rose flounces off, followed by the others

Queen Honestly. Have you ever seen anything like it? Oh, they're not like
the fairies *we* were when I was her age. Still—why worry? Folk aren't wish-
ing for things like they used to do, so there's nothing for us to do but eat
and get fat. (*She grimaces*) And who wants fairies who are fair, fat and forty?

SONG 11

At the end of the song there is a flurry of Fairies entering

*The Fairies dash into their positions and strike poses. Queen Snowdrift smoothes
down her hair, dress, etc.*

David, Mary and the Sprite enter

Rose Okay, girls. Routine five.

*In very out-of-tune voices, they lurch into a spirited rendering of "Nymphs and
Shepherds". Queen Snowdrift reels under the onslaught, and winces.*

Queen Oooooooooh. Stop. I surrender.

The voices trail off

I'll strangle that choirmaster. (*Raising a fixed smile, she faces the visitors*)
Greetings, dear mortals, and welcome to our Fairy Glade. I am Queen
Snowdrift. (*She curtsies low, and her joints lock*) Oooh. (*She totters bent
double to her Throne and sits*)
David Thank you, your—er—your Majesty.
Queen And what can I do you for? (*She corrects herself*) Er—do for you?
(*She waves her wand haphazardly*)
Sprite They have come to ask for your help, O mighty Queen.
Queen Oh, dear—and I haven't read a teacup in years. Still—if you cross my
palm with sil ...
Mary No, no, your Majesty. We're trying to stop the Wizard of Bong from
stealing the Jewel of Miracles.

All the Fairies take notice

Queen (*interested*) Are you, *really*? (*She shrugs*) Well, I don't think there's
anything to be ... (*She realizes*) Trying to do *what*??

David Stop the Wizard of Bong from stealing the Jewel of Miracles.
Queen (*rising*) But he *can't*. I won't allow it. How dare he set foot in my Fairy Kingdom? Who brought him here?
Sprite The Black Imp, your Majesty.
Queen The Black Imp? Nonsense. Impossible. I clocked him in the lock—er—locked him in the Clock.
David But the Wizard has freed him, your Majesty, and they intend to steal the Jewel and destroy you all.

The Fairies all look aghast

Mary They must have reached the Enchanted Lake by now.
Queen Oh, this is terrible. We must hurry. You three dash off and warn King Neptune, while I get ready for the battle. Tell the old boy I sent you, and to expect me within the hour.
Sprite But your Majesty. Aren't you forgetting something?
Queen (*raising her eyebrows in question, then remembering*) Oh, yes. Of course. The mortals can't breathe underwater, can they? Never mind. (*She fiddles with her stocking tops and fishes out two lozenges*) Take these Magic Lozenges, and suck them just before you go into the water. (*She peers at them*) Oh—not *that* one. It's a sherbert sucker. Just a minute. (*She fiddles in her stocking tops again*) Here we are. (*She produces another lozenge and hands them over*) Quickly now. There's not a moment to lose.

David, Mary and the Sprite exit right

(*To the Fairies*) Sound the alarm. Ring all the bluebells.

All exit in alarm and confusion. As soon as the noise dies away, Dame Foxtrot and Willie enter cautiously

Willie Are you sure this is where the Fairy Queen lives?
Dame Well, that's what the *Pixies* told us, isn't it? (*She sees the throne*) Of course it is. Can't you see the throne?
Willie (*looking at it*) Yes, but unless she's very thin, I don't think she's at home.
Dame (*looking around*) It certainly is quiet.

There is a loud bump, off

Whassat??
Willie What time is it?
Dame Half-past eight.
Willie Then it must have been night falling.
Dame Oh—and talking about falling ... (*She flutters her eyes at him*)
Willie Oh, not again, Gerty. Don't you ever think of anything else but getting engaged?
Dame Of course I do. Getting married. (*All romantic*) Oh, Willie. Take me in your arms and kiss me fervently.
Willie Oh, all right. Where is it?
Dame (*with great drama*) Don't you realize you're exactly my kind of man.
Willie (*pleased*) Am I?

Dame Yes—you're *alive*. (*With great emphasis*) Well??
Willie Well what?
Dame Are you going to kiss me, or aren't you?
Willie (*unenthusiastically*) I suppose so.
Dame (*coyly*) Don't you dare, or I'll scream.
Willie Oh, come here. (*He grabs her*)

SONG 12

Queen Snowdrift and the Fairies enter, armed for battle

Queen Oh, more of them. (*Graciously*) Welcome to the Fairy Glade.
Willie Are you a fairy? You don't look it.
Queen Are you a mortal? *You* don't look it.
Dame I've never seen a fairy like *you* before.
Queen Have you ever seen a fairy before?
Dame Well—no.
Queen Then how do you know what a fairy looks like, then?
Willie (*laughing*) That's one in the eye for you, Gerty.
Dame Yes, and there'll be one in the eye for you, in a minute. (*To the Queen*) Who's this little lot, then?
Queen (*waving her wand*) This is my fairy band.
Willie Oh—are they going to play something for us?
Queen (*indicating them*) Rose, Lily, Poppy, Iris, Daisy, etc.
Willie Proper little flower garden, isn't it?
Queen *And* I have a Dewdrop.
Dame Well use your handkerchief.

The Fairies giggle

Slap and Tickle enter

Queen (*turning to them*) Welcome to our Fairy Glade, dear mortals.
Willie They aren't dear mortals—they're *cheap* ones.
Queen (*rotating her wand*) Advance and state your request.
Slap Eh?
Tickle (*blankly*) Do what?
Queen (*rolling her eyes in despair*) What do you want, darling?
Dame They don't want anything. They're following us.
Queen (*to the Dame*) And where are *you* going?
Dame I'm trying to rescue my little girl Mary from the Blizzard of Song, and Willie's helping me.
Queen Oh, well—I think *I* can put your mind at rest about *that*. She's just been rescued by her young man and one of my Immortals, and they've all gone to the Court of King Neptune.
Dame You mean she's safe?
Queen Safe as *houses*. The only thing is, the rest of us are in frightful danger. That dreadful Wizard is trying to steal our Jewel of Miracles, and unless we get to King Neptune in time, we've had our chips.
Willie In that case, Dame Foxtrot had better come with you. *And* these two. (*He indicates Slap and Tickle*)

Slap Here, just a minute. What about you?

Tickle Yes. What are *you* going to do?

Willie I'm going to stay here and finish my homework.

Dame What homework? You left school, *years* ago.

Willie I know, but I'm a very slow writer.

Dame Yes, but if you don't come along with us, you'll be able to boast that
you wrote your own death warrant at top speed.

The Baron, the Baroness and Herbert enter

Queen (*startled*) Good Heavens. *More* of them. (*She gives a light laugh*) To
what do I owe the pleasure of this unexpurgated visit? Is there a coach trip
in? (*She waves her wand*) Queen Snowdrift at your service. (*She spots
Herbert*) Oh—I'm *terribly* sorry my dears, but pets aren't allowed in the
Fairy Glade. Trade Union rules, you know.

Baroness Pets?? What's the woman talking about? We've got no pets with
us.

Queen What about that one? (*She indicates Herbert*)

Herbert I'm not a *pet*. I'm *Herbert*, their son.

Queen (*confused*) Oh, I'm terribly sorry.

Baron (*snarling*) So are we.

Baroness What's going on here, anyway?

Queen We're going to defend the Jewel of Miracles from the nasty old Wizard
of Bong. Would you like to come along with us. The more the merrier,
as they say.

Baron (*his eyes lighting up*) You're going to where the Jewels are? Then of
course we'll come, won't we, my dear?

Baroness With pleasure.

Queen Right. Off we go.

*The Queen moves right, followed by all the mortals. The Fairies remain where
they are*

Girls. *Girls*. I said, "Off we go".

Rose Off *you* go, Queenie. We're staying here. You've got a *strike* on your
hands, you have.

Dame A strike? In this place?

Queen (*with a sigh*) Yes, I'm afraid my fairies are revolting.

Herbert And you can certainly say that again.

Rose (*grimly*) Right, that's done it. Come on, girls. Everybody out.

All the Fairies exit

Willie Oh, that's torn it.

Queen (*airily*) Not at all. I've *just* thought of a plan. Gather round and I'll
tell it to you.

They all go into a huddle for a moment, then separate again

Now off you go—and remember. It all depends on you.

Dame But what if something goes wrong?

Queen Oh, I don't think it *will*.

Everyone except the Queen exits right

But just in case it *does*. (*She lifts the seat of the Throne and lifts out a telephone. She dials a number*) Hello? Is that——(*she mentions a local travel office*)? I wonder if you could give me some information about plane tickets to Australia?

The Lights fade to a BLACKOUT *and the inner curtains close*

SCENE 4

By the Enchanted Lake

The Wizard and the Imp enter left

Wizard Here we are at last. The Enchanted Lake lies before us, and the Jewel of Miracles waits beneath it. Soon it will be mine and I shall be ruler of the Universe. (*He laughs*)

Imp And what about me?

Wizard Oh, yes. I'd forgotten about *you*. (*He smiles*) But never mind. I'm sure I can think of *something*.

Imp I didn't like the way you said that. If you think you can trick me, you'd better think again. My powers are just as strong as yours.

Wizard Trick you? My dear Imp—I wouldn't try to trick you out of anything. After all you've helped me a lot.

Imp Yes—well don't you forget it.

Wizard (*aside*) The stupid fool. Once the Jewel is mine, I'll soon dispose of him. (*Aloud*) Come then. There's no time to be lost.

Imp (*suddenly*) Wait—someone's coming.

Wizard (*looking off left*) It's the Sprite and two of the mortals. Hide.

Imp Are we going to kill them?

Wizard No, you fool. I want them to get ahead of us. Now move before they see you.

The Wizard and the Imp hide off right. The Sprite, David and Mary enter left

Sprite Now wait here for a moment whilst I check that the coast is clear. And remember, this will be our only chance.

The Sprite exits right

David I wonder where the Wizard is now. And the Imp.

Mary I don't know, but I hope it's nowhere near here.

David Why? You're not afraid, are you?

Mary A little. Aren't you?

David No fear. I can deal with them.

Mary You seem very sure of yourself.

David Better sure than sorry, and I've got nothing to be sorry about. I have you back again, and that's all I need to give me courage.

SONG 13

After the song, the Sprite enters

Sprite Quickly now.

> *David, Mary and the Sprite exit right. As soon as they have gone, the Wizard and Imp emerge*

Wizard (*with a smile*) That's right. Hurry along, my little ones. The faster you travel, the faster the Jewel will be in my hands. (*He roars with laughter*) Come. To the Kingdom of King Neptune.

> *The Wizard and the Imp exit as the Lights fade and the Curtains open*

SCENE 5

The Court of King Neptune

A most spectacular scene. King Neptune is seated on his shell Throne up centre, and one of his Mermaids sits at the side of him on the floor. A huge chest with jewels spilling out of it is right, and a smaller one is to one side of it, full of gold coins. A stand topped by a velvet cushion is far right, and the massive Jewel of Miracles rests on it, well lit. Water Spirits, male and female, perform a ballet beneath the draped nets and starfish, etc., that form the top of the Court

> *After the ballet, David and Mary enter*

Neptune (*surprised*) Welcome to the Court of King Neptune.

The Water Spirits withdraw into the background

David Thank you, your Majesty. But I'm afraid we bring you bad news.
Neptune (*surprised*) What? You dare to bring bad news on our holiday?
Mary We're sorry, but it can't be helped. You are all in terrible danger. The Wizard of Bong is planning to steal the Jewel of Miracles.

There is an excited flurry from the Water spirits

Neptune (*amused*) Steal the Jewel? (*He laughs*) Oh, dear, oh dear. And however do you think he's going to manage *that*? Why—he'd *have* to come right into this very room to even *see* it. Look—there it lies on yonder stand. (*He points to it*)
David (*surprised*) Is it *safe* there?
Neptune Safe? (*He laughs*) It's safe as Davy Jones' Locker. Just try to touch it. Go on.

David moves towards the stand. Two armed Water Spirits spring on to the stage, their tridents aimed at him. He stops moving

You see? (*He waves the guardians away*)

The armed Water Spirits exit

No-one but me can lay a finger on it. (*He moves to the stand and lifts the Jewel*) Have you ever *seen* a Jewel such as this before? Not only is it the largest precious stone ever found, but its powers of Magic are quite

unbelievable. That's why we keep it down here. It wouldn't do to let the wrong kind of person get hold of it, would it? (*He hands the Jewel to David*)
David (*taking it*) It's beautiful. (*He shows it to Mary*)
Mary (*worried*) Oh, please put it back where it's safe, your Majesty. If the Wizard comes in now, he can take it without any trouble.
Neptune (*smiling as he takes back the Jewel*) Ah, don't you worry about that, young lady. I may be an old man, but I've still got my wits about me. It would take more than the Wizard of Bong, whoever *he* is, to get the better of me. (*He replaces the Jewel*) Still—it was very kind of you to come and warn me, even though it *was* a bit of a wasted journey. But I'll make it up to you. Go into the other cave—(*He points*)—and help yourselves to a few pearls and things.
Mary Oh, we *couldn't*.
Neptune Of course you could. I never knew a woman yet who could resist pretty jewellery. Go on. Off you go, and when you get back, we'll have a little party or something. We haven't had visitors down here for centuries.
David Oh—that reminds me. Queen Snowdrift of the Fairies is on her way here too.
Neptune What? Old Theory?
Mary Theory? Is that her name?
Neptune Not really, but that's what we call her down here.
David Why's that?
Neptune She hardly ever works. (*He laughs hugely*)

David and Mary exit into the other cave

(*To his Court*) Did you hear that, everyone? Old Snowdrift's on her way down here. Looking for a husband again, I shouldn't wonder. Hope she doesn't think *I'm* going to propose to her. (*He laughs*) No, a bachelor I am, and a bachelor I'm going to stay. Quite frankly, I find women a bit of a problem—but they're just the kind of problems I like wrestling with.

SONG 14

After the song, the Wizard enters in disguise

Wizard Greetings, your Majesty. (*He bows*)
Neptune (*turning*) And greetings to you, sir. Welcome to my Kingdom.
Wizard I come from your good friend Queen Snowdrift of the Fairies, and bring you an urgent message.
Neptune (*puzzled*) Another one?
Wizard (*in mock horror*) You mean—I'm *too late*?
Neptune For what?
Wizard To warn you that the Wizard of Bong is trying to steal the Jewel of Miracles.
Neptune (*bewildered*) But I know. The other two just told me. The young man and the girl.
Wizard (*with a loud wail*) The young man and the girl. (*With heavy drama*) Your Majesty—you've been *tricked*. The young man *is* the Wizard, and the girl his accomplice. (*He groans*) Ohhhhhh, they've stolen the Jewel.

Neptune No they haven't. It's over there. Look (*He points*)
Wizard Ah—but is that the *real* Jewel? If the Wizard only touched it for a
moment, he would have changed it for an imitation.
Neptune (*aghast*) Oh, my goodness. I actually *gave* it to him to hold. (*He
hurries to the stand and gets the Jewel*) I'll examine it at once. (*He peers
at it*) It *seems* to be the same one.
Wizard (*holding out his hands*) Let me see. Let *me* see.
Neptune (*peering closely*) Yes, I'm *sure* it's the right one. But perhaps I'd better
try it to be certain.
Wizard (*quickly*) No. Let *me* see it.
Neptune It won't take a moment.
Wizard (*harshly*) Give it to *me*, you doddering old fool.
Neptune (*startled*) Eh?

> *Mary and David enter. Mary holds jewels, David carries a silver sword. They
> see what is happening*

David (*urgently*) The Wizard.
Mary Look out.
Wizard (*snatching the Jewel*) Too late. The Jewel is *mine*.
David (*lifting the sword*) But not for long.
Wizard (*holding up the Jewel*) Stand back. I command you to fall into an
enchanted sleep.

> *David collapses on the floor*

Mary David. (*She kneels beside him*)
Neptune (*to the Wizard*) You shall suffer for this. The Spirits of the Lake will
rise against you.
Wizard (*sneering*) Bah, they can do nothing whilst I have the Jewel. From
now on, *I* rule the Enchanted Lake, and you are my slaves. (*He holds aloft
the Jewel*) Take these carrion away.

> *The Water Spirits take David, Mary and King Neptune off*

Now let us have feasting and dancing to celebrate my victory. Send in the
Water Nymphs.

> *Dame Foxtrot, Willie, the Baron, the Baroness, Slap, Tickle, Herbert and
> the Fairy Queen enter as Water Nymphs*

> *They perform a Balloon Ballet. At the end of the Ballet, the Wizard applauds.
> All make a dash for the Jewel, but the Wizard grabs it and holds it aloft.*

So—you thought you could trick me out of my *prize*, did you? Steal my
Jewel. Well, I have *news* for you.
Dame And I've got some for you. A man swallowed a dud coin last night,
and he's expected to be charged later today with passing counterfeit money.
Wizard Silence, you old witch.
Willie Here, don't you call the old witch an old witch, or I'll dot you one.
Wizard Shut up, you idiotic, half-brained, bow-legged, knock-kneed nin-
compoop.

Willie (*shrugging*) Nobody's perfect.
Wizard (*with great menace*) You are all in my power, and will die very, very slowly.
Slap Huh. Another one on a go-slow.
Wizard (*furiously*) Shut up. Shut up. Shut up.
Tickle (*in posh tones*) That was a repeat performance.
Wizard Prepare to die.
Queen Just a minute. You can't kill me. I'm Queen Snowdrift.
Wizard Queen Snowdrift, eh? (*He laughs*) Well stand by for some warm weather.
Queen (*raising her wand*) To the death ...

The Black Imp springs on to the stage and snatches the wand from her hand

Oooooh.
Imp I have it. The Fairy Queen is helpless.
Queen Oh, you little squirt. Give it here at once.
Imp Not likely.
Herbert Do as you're told, Inkblot. (*He snatches the wand*)
Imp (*tugging*) Let go.
Baroness Herbert ... (*She rushes to help him*)
Wizard (*loudly*) Stop. I command you all to freeze solid.

Everyone but the Imp goes rigid

Fools. You'll remain like that *for ever*.
Imp For ever?
Wizard Until the end of time itself. Nothing is immune from the power of the Jewel, as well you know.
Imp Except, of course, a person without a brain.
Wizard (*shrugging*) Come. Let's get out of this Lake and into the normal world again. This place gives me the creeps with all its weeds and shadows. Now that the Jewel is in my hands, I shall rule the Universe.

The Wizard laughs and exits. The Imp follows

The frozen figures remain as they were for a moment, then Dame Foxtrot's head moves

Dame They've gone.

The others all unfreeze

Baroness Did you hear what he said? That Jewel worked on anything except a person without a brain.
Baron Yes. Aren't we lucky?
Tickle He said he was going to rule the Universe.
Willie He couldn't Rule Britannia, never mind the Universe.

Mary and King Neptune enter

Mary Mother.
Dame Oh, Daughter. (*They embrace*) But where's David, and who's this?

Neptune I am King Neptune, and David is in the cave back there. We can't waken him.

Mary The Wizard put a spell on him, and now he's going to sleep for ever.

Queen Oh no, he isn't. A quick wave of my rusty—I mean trusty wand, and we'll have him back on his feet in no time.

Neptune Splendid.

Queen Oh, wait. I've just remembered. I can't. That nasty old Imp has swiped it, and I haven't brought a spare.

The Sprite enters

Sprite Then use mine, your Majesty. (*She offers her wand to the Queen*)

Queen Oh, *thanks*, love. (*She takes it*) I'll make you a Dame for this.

Sprite (*looking at Dame Foxtrot askance*) Oh, I don't think *that's* necessary, your Majesty.

Mary It's this way.

Mary leads Queen Snowdrift, Neptune and the Sprite off

Baron Now's our chance. Look at the gold lying about here. We're *rich*.

Baroness (*looking off*) Over there, too. There's a cave *full* of it.

Slap Come on. Let's start collecting.

Tickle Yippee.

Slap and Tickle dash off, followed by the Baron, the Baroness and Herbert

Willie (*eagerly*) Come on, Gerty.

Dame Just a minute. Just a minute. You're going nowhere.

Willie But what about the gold?

Dame Never mind the gold. What use is it if the bearded wonder's going to be the ruler of the Universe? He'll just take it all off us, won't he?

Willie Oh—I never thought of that.

Dame So while they're wasting their time out there, we can have a little sit down and talk about our wedding plans. (*She sits on the throne and pats the seat beside her*) Now come on ... and don't tread on the goldfish. (*She smiles at the Mermaid*)

Willie (*sitting beside her*) All right.

Dame Now then—before we start, let's get a bit more comfy. (*She snuggles closer to him*) I wouldn't object if you wanted to put your arm round me, you know.

Willie Wouldn't you?

Dame Not a bit.

The arm of an Octopus slides from behind the throne and wraps itself around her waist

Mmmmmm. That's better.

Willie looks blankly out front and blinks

Oooooh, you aren't half strong. (*She giggles*)

Another arm comes out and wraps round Willie

Willie Oooooooh. So are you.

Dame (*after a slight frown*) You know—your arm feels ever so smooth. (*She strokes it*)

Willie (*feeling the arm around him*) So does yours.

Another arm comes over the back of the throne and between them

Dame Hey—stop it, you saucepot. That tickles.

Willie What does?

Dame *That* does. (*She giggles*)

Willie But I'm not doing anything.

Another arm comes over the back of the throne and touches Willie

Eh? (*He sees the arm*) You see. It's not me at all. It's something all long and green.

Dame (*looking down at the arm holding her*) Oh, so it is. It looks just like one of them octopusseries.

Willie (*weakly*) I think it *is* one of them octopusseries.

With loud shrieks, they leap up from the throne

David, Mary and the Sprite enter.

Sprite Quickly. Call the others. David is recovered now, and we have one final chance to recover the Jewel. We must return to the Clock and make it strike again.

Dame Why?

David According to the Fairy Queen, if the clock strikes a *second* time, the Imp will be whisked back into it, and his powers will vanish.

Willie But what about the Wizard?

Mary With any luck, we won't have anything to fear from him, either.

Sprite Only an Immortal can carry the Jewel out of the Never-Never Land, and into the world of Mortals. That means he will *have* to let the Imp take it through for him. If we can make the Clock strike whilst the Imp is still holding it, *I* can deal with him before he has time to use it himself.

Dame Then what are we waiting for. Come on.

The lights fade to a BLACKOUT, *and the curtains close quickly*

SCENE 6

A pathway

The Wizard enters right, laughing

Wizard Mine. All mine. (*He gloats over the Jewel*) I'll show those stupid immortals who's the boss now. And as for the fools back on *Earth*—I've got plans for them too. (*He laughs and moves left to exit, but is flung back as if by an invisible hand*) What?? (*He tries to leave again, but is stopped*)

The Black Imp enters right

Imp (*amused*) Having trouble?

Wizard (*turning with a snarl*) Not as long as I hold *this*. (*He raises the Jewel*)

Imp It won't do you any good. That's the one thing the Jewel *can't* help you with. Only an Immortal can take it out of *this* place. It's a kind of safety measure.

Wizard Is it, indeed? (*He smiles*) But there's nothing to stop *you* taking it through for me, is there?

Imp Nothing in the world.

Wizard (*thrusting the Jewel at him*) Then take it.

The Imp takes the Jewel

After you.

The Imp exits left

Wizard (*glaring after him*) The little fool. Does he think I'm going to share my powers with him? (*He laughs*) Once on the other side, I'll soon dispense with *his* services.

The Wizard laughs and exits left. David, Mary, and the Sprite enter right

Sprite Quickly.

David, Mary and the Sprite exit left. The Dame, Willie, the Baron, the Baroness, Herbert, Slap and Tickle enter right in confusion. They exit left. Queen Snowdrift and King Neptune enter right, out of breath

Neptune (*panting*) It's no use. I can't go any further.

Queen (*gasping*) Me neither. I haven't dashed around like this in years.

Neptune (*gazing off left*) Well, there they go. Let's hope they arrive in time.

Queen Oh, don't mention time to me. If I hadn't locked that nasty little Imp inside that Clock, none of this would have happened.

Neptune Now, now, Snowdrift. Don't go getting yourself all upset. You weren't to know, were you, and I suppose it seemed a good idea at the moment.

Queen (*sadly*) It did. But I should have known better. After all. I am the Fairy Queen—or at least I *was*. (*Her face crumpling*) Oh, Neppy. I'm a failure. I've lost me magic wand. Me fairies are on strike, and now I've let the Wizard pinch the Jewel. (*She sobs*)

Neptune Yes, it has been a funny sort of day for you, hasn't it? Still—never mind. If the worst comes to the worst, you can always come and stay with me. After all—we've been friends for a long, long while, haven't we?

Queen (*cheering up slightly*) I suppose we have. And we've shared a few laughs as well—back in the good old days.

Neptune (*chuckling*) I'll say. And if things don't work out right, we'll try to share a few more in the bad ones to come. And who knows. In a few more years, the good times may come back again and we can laugh at the *lot*, eh?

Queen We can try.

SONG 15

At the end of the song, the Lights fade to a BLACKOUT *and the curtains open*

SCENE 7

The village square

The Clock stands up centre. The Villagers are once more singing and dancing

SONG 16

At the end of the song, the door of the Clock flies open and the Imp emerges. The Villagers flee in terror. The Wizard emerges

Wizard (*as he enters*) Quickly. The Jewel. Give it to me.
Imp (*backing slightly*) Wait. What do *I* get?
Wizard The Jewel first, *then* I'll give you your reward.
Imp Oh, no. I don't trust you. I think you mean to trick me.
Wizard Don't be such a fool. Give me the Jewel.
Imp No.
Wizard (*snarling with rage*) I'm warning you.
Imp (*defiantly*) You cannot harm me. My powers are just as strong as yours. And besides—*I* have the Jewel.
Wizard Yes, but you cannot *use* it. Only a mortal can use it on this side of the Clock.
Imp I don't believe you. (*He looks down at it*)
Wizard (*grabbing it*) Aha.
Imp (*struggling with him*) Let go.

As they wrestle for possession, the Jewel slips out of the Imp's grasp, and shoots off left

Wizard (*horrified*) My Jewel!

The Wizard dashes off left, pursued by the Imp. As they exit, David, Mary and the Sprite enter from the Clock

David (*looking off left*) There they go.
Mary Quick. Start up the Clock again.
Sprite No—not until the Imp has the Jewel, or all will be in vain. Follow them and wait for the right moment, whilst I warn my companion Sprites to get ready to seize him.

The Sprite exits right

David And once *he's* out of the way, *I've* got a little score to settle with the Wizard of Bong.

David and Mary exit left. As they go, the Dame and Willie enter from the Clock

Willie Look. There's nobody here. They can't have arrived yet.
Dame What do you mean, they can't have arrived yet? They're all in front of us. Look in the house. Maybe they're in there.

Willie dashes off into the cottage

(*To the audience*) Oh, I hope we're not too late. I don't fancy being a slave for the rest of me life. Not to that Wizard, anyway. He's the kind of person you only like to run in to when he's walking, and you're driving a fast car.

Willie rushes back

Willie There's nobody there. It's empty—except for big heaps of dust all over the place.

Dame Big heaps of dust? In my cottage? *Never.*

Willie But there is, Gerty. We must have been away for weeks. The dust is so thick the spiders are walking about on stilts.

Dame (*gasping*) Ohhhhhh. (*With a start*) Look out. There's somebody coming. Hide.

The Dame and Willie hide behind the Clock

Slap and Tickle emerge from inside it

Slap Quick, quick.

Tickle (*protesting*) I'm being as quick as I can. I'm not used to all this dashing about, you know.

Slap Huh. And you can say that again. The only exercise you get lately is watching horror films and letting your flesh creep.

Tickle Oh, yes? And what about *you*? Swallowed a teaspoon ten years ago, and haven't bothered to stir since.

Slap Har, har. Very funny. Well just for that, I'll start the Clock on my own.

Dame (*emerging from behind the Clock*) Oh, no you won't. Me and Willie were here first. *We're* going to start the Clock.

Willie Right. So you two can go take a running jump.

Tickle (*drawing himself up*) Sez who?

Dame (*drawing herself up*) Sez *me*.

Slap Huh, we're not scared of you, you old has-been.

Dame Has-been? *Has-been?* Don't you call *me* a has-been, you pop-eyed pilferer. For your inflammation, I'm not even a never-wazzar. And besides, I hate that word, old.

Tickle I'm not surprised. You're so ancient, you can remember Madam Butterfly when she was a caterpillar.

Willie I beg your pardon. My Gerty's only just over the age of consent.

Slap Yes, but she's heading for the age of *collapse*.

Dame I'll collapse *you*, in a minute ... (*She rolls up her sleeves*)

Willie (*suddenly*) Look out. Somebody's coming out of the Clock.

Everyone rushes to hide behind the Clock

The Baron and Baroness enter from it

Baroness (*angrily*) I never want to see another Clock in my life. All this charging about, and not a solitary diamond to show for it. Why did we have to leave before we had time to fill our pockets?

Baron It was all that stupid Sprite's fault. We could have been millionaires by now, if it hadn't been for her. Who cares about the Wizard and that idiotic Jewel? We were *cheated*. (*He turns and kicks the Clock angrily*) Owwwwwww. (*He hops about on one foot*)

Baroness (*startled*) Archibald—it's started ticking again.

The Wizard comes scuttling in left, clutching the Jewel to him. He cannons into the Baron and drops it

Wizard The Jewel. (*He makes a dive for it*)
Baroness (*kicking him up the bottom*) Get off.
Baron (*rushing forward and seizing it*) I've got it. I've got it. I've got the Jewel.

The Black Imp enters with a bound

Imp Give that to *me*. It's mine.
Baron Oh. Sorry. (*He holds it out*)

Before the Imp can take the Jewel, Willie dashes out from behind the Clock and snatches it, continuing running until he cannons into the Wizard getting up

Willie Oo-er.

As the Wizard makes a grab for him, Willie turns and tosses the Jewel to Dame Foxtrot who follows him out of hiding with the others

Gerty.
Dame (*catching it*) Aaaaaaah.

The Imp dashes towards her, and she tosses it to Tickle. He in turn passes it to Baroness as the Wizard rushes at him

Baroness It's mine.

The Imp rushes towards her, and she tosses it to the Wizard, who by this time is by the Clock

(*realizing*) Oooooooh.
Wizard (*in triumph*) Ahaaaaaaaa. (*He holds the Jewel aloft*) It's *mine*.

Herbert pops out of the Clock and calmly takes the Jewel out of the Wizard's hands

Herbert *Thank* you.
Baron Herbert!
Wizard (*snarling*) Give that to me.
Herbert Not until you say please.
Wizard Very well then—*please*. (*He holds out his hand eagerly*)
Herbert Let's have a little smile with it, too.
Wizard (*giving him a hideous false smile*) PLEASE. Now hand it over, you
    dim-witted dolt.
Herbert. Sharnt. (*He sticks his tongue out at the Wizard*)

Herbert turns to grin at his parents, and the Imp springs and snatches the Jewel

Imp (*crowing with delight*) It's mine. It's mine. At last it's *mine*.

David and Mary enter. A sword is fastened to David's waist

David But not for long.

Grabbing the Wizard's arm, David propels him in a half-circle, backwards, to crash into the Clock. The shock makes it strike

Imp (*in a fury*) No. No. I won't go back. I *won't*.

Drawn by invisible threads, the Imp is dragged back into the Clock, fighting and screaming. The door closes behind him and his cries fade

Wizard (*staggering back*) Curses. I must fly. But I'll return for my revenge.
David Not so fast, you mystical maggot. This time you're going to pay for all the trouble you've caused. (*He draws his sword*)
Wizard You would not fight an unarmed man.
David Choose your weapon.
Wizard Very well. (*He edges close to Mary*) I'll take *this* one. (*He grabs Mary*) *Now* let's see you try to stop me. One move and the girl dies.
Mary Don't listen to him, David. Stop him.
Wizard (*edging back to the Clock, dragging Mary with him*) Remember. Just one step, and she's finished.

The door of the Clock opens and Queen Snowdrift enters with her wand

Queen (*beaming*) And so are *you*. (*She taps him with her wand*)

The Wizard goes rigid. Mary breaks free and runs to David

Like the U.S. Cavalry, I've arrived in time. We've fixed the Black Imp, and got me magic wand back; Neppy's taken the Jewel home with him again, and the Fairies have accepted a ten per cent pay rise, so the strike's over and everything's back to normal.
Dame What did you do to him. The Black Imp?
Queen I've turned him into something that's no use to anybody.
Willie What's that?
Queen A politician. (*She looks at the Wizard*) And now—let's think what I'm going to do with *this* one.
Wizard (*still frozen*) Mercy. Don't kill me.
Queen Kill you? Oh, no. I'm not going to *kill* you. I've got *other* plans for *you*. I've been thinking about getting *married* again and it just occurred to me ...
Wizard (*wailing*) No. Not that. Not that. Kill me, instead.
Queen (*brightly*) Come along, Wizzy. I'm sure you'll make a wonderful husband. (*She taps him with her wand*)
Wizard (*being drawn into the Clock*) Help me, somebody. *Help me.*
Queen Bye-bye, everybody. Thanks for everything.

The Queen follows the Wizard into the Clock and the door closes

David (*laughing*) It looks like the Wizard's reign of terror is over.
Mary And the Fairy Queen's is just beginning.
Baron That's all very well. But what about us?
Baroness All the work *we* did, and we don't have anything to show for it.
Herbert Oh, yes we do. I filled my pockets before we left that cave.
Baron My *wonderful* little boy. (*He hugs him*) What did you get? Gold, diamonds or pearls?
Herbert Oh, no. Nothing like that. I got these smashing sea shells. (*He digs in his pocket for them*)

Baroness Idiot. Fool. Dolt. Blockhead.

The Baron and the Baroness chase Herbert off, trying to do him an injury

Dame So we're right back where we started from. Poor but happy.

Mary Not quite, mother. King Neptune gave *me* enough jewellery to keep us in luxury for the rest of our lives.

Willie And I got *one* little souvenir. (*He produces an immense diamond ring which he slips on to Dame Foxtrot's finger*)

Slap
Tickle } (*producing handfuls of gold coins*) Us, too. {*Speaking together*}

David Then all's well that ends well, and from now on, may our past misunderstandings be forgotten, and let's all live happily ever after.

All cheer, then move forward to sing

SONG 17

During the song, the inner curtains close behind them

At the end of the song, all exit left and right

The Lights fade to a BLACKOUT, *and rise again almost at once*

FINALE

Dickory Dock Mansion

The cast assemble in the following order:

> Juniors in their Mice costumes
> Townsfolk
> Neptune and Queen Snowdrift
> The Black Imp and the Wizard
> The Sprite
> The Baron, the Baroness and Herbert
> Slap and Tickle
> The Dame and Willie
> Mary and David

When the whole cast is assembled, the Sprite steps forward

Sprite And now the tale is over, for good has won the day.
The Imp and Wizard beaten. The cast have shown the way.
So now we bid you all "Good night" and hope you will not mock
Our efforts to amuse you—with Hickory, Dickory Dock.

Reprise of any song in the show which is considered suitable

CURTAIN

FURNITURE AND PROPERTY LIST

ACT I

Scene 1

On stage: **Dame's** cottage cut-out

Off stage: Broom **(Dame)**
2 chairs **(Slap, Tickle)**

Personal: **Baron:** whip
David: purse of coins

Scene 2

On stage: Nil

Off stage: Key **(Wizard)**

Personal: **Dame:** sheet of paper, pound note
Willie: pencil

Scene 3

On stage: Table with cloth concealing trick top and plastic bucket under to catch
tea. *On it:* large canteen teapot, 2 small cups—one with hole in bottom,
2 small saucers—one with hole in bottom, 2 plates of fish and chips,
cutlery, crockery as dressing
2 chairs
Grandfather clock. *In it:* buckets, pans, dishes, brooms. *Behind it:* giant
mousetrap

Off stage: Sauce bottle **(Willie)**
2 blankets **(Willie)**
Burglar kits, sack of tools, etc. **(Slap, Tickle)**
Alarm clock **(Tickle)**

Personal: **Wizard:** gold coins

Scene 4

On stage: Nil

Off stage: Mousetraps **(Dancers)**

Scene 5

On stage: Grandfather Clock (hands set at almost one)

Off stage: Shotgun **(Dame)**
2 policeman's helmets, 2 truncheons **(Slap, Tickle)**

Scene 6

On stage: Nil

Off stage: Candles **(Choristers)**

56

Scene 7

On stage: As Scene 1

Off stage: Shopping basket with chicken hanging out (**Dame**)
2 glasses of brandy (**Boy**)

ACT II

Scene 1

On stage: *On floor:* shoe's inner sole, Square of white tissue paper

Off stage: Garlands of flowers (**Elves, Pixies**)

Personal: **Sprite:** wand

Scene 2

On stage: Nil

Scene 3

On stage: **Fairy Queen's** throne, with false wings and tiara attached. *Inside seat:* telephone

Off stage: Garlands of flowers (**Fairies**)
"Arms for battle" (**Fairies**)

Personal: **Fairy Queen:** "wilted wand", several lozenges in stocking tops

Scene 4

On stage: Nil

Scene 5

On stage: Draped nets
Shell throne
Large chest of jewels
Small chest of coins
Stand with velvet cushion and "Jewel of Miracles"

Off stage: 2 tridents (**Water Spirits**)
Jewels (**Mary**)
Silver sword (**David**)
Balloons (**Balloon Ballet Dancers**)

Scene 6

On stage: Nil

Scene 7

On stage: As Act I Scene 1, with Grandfather Clock up C

Off stage: Sea shells (**Herbert**)
Diamond ring (**Willie**)
Handfuls of coins (**Slap, Tickle**)

LIGHTING PLOT

Property fittings required: nil

Various simple settings on open stage

ACT I

To open:	Bright overall lighting	
Cue 1	At end of Scene 1	(Page 8)
	Cross-fade to front stage lighting	
Cue 2	At end of Scene 2	(Page 14)
	Cross-fade to **Dame's** cottage, interior	
Cue 3	At end of SONG 5	(Page 17)
	Lights dim slightly	
Cue 4	At end of Scene 3	(Page 19)
	Cross-fade to front stage lighting	
Cue 5	At end of Mouse Dance	(Page 20)
	Cross-fade to Dickory Dock Mansion lighting	
Cue 6	At end of Scene 5	(Page 24)
	Cross-fade to front stage lighting	
Cue 7	At end of "Night" dance	(Page 25)
	Cross-fade to opening lighting, Scene 1	

ACT II

To open:	Bright overall lighting	
Cue 8	**Wizard:** "Enjoy your 'rest'."	(Page 31)
	Fade to spot on **Mary**	
Cue 9	At end of SONG 9	(Page 32)
	Return to previous lighting	
Cue 10	**Sprite:** "Begone!"	(Page 33)
	Beam of white light on **Imp:** *retain until* **Sprite** *waves her wand*	
Cue 11	At end of Scene 1	(Page 37)
	Cross-fade to front stage lighting	
Cue 12	At end of Scene 2	(Page 37)
	Cross-fade to Fairy Glen lighting	
Cue 13	**Queen:** "... plane tickets to Australia?"	(Page 43)
	Fade to BLACKOUT, *then up to front stage lighting*	
Cue 14	At end of Scene 4	(Page 44)
	Cross-fade to **Neptune's** Court lighting, with spotlight on Jewel of Miracles	

Lighting Plot   59

Cue 15   **Dame** "Come on"   (Page 49)
             BLACKOUT, *then up to front stage lighting*
Cue 16   At end of SONG 15   (Page 50)
             Fade to BLACKOUT, *then up to overall lighting, Village Square*
Cue 17   At end of SONG 17   (Page 55)
             Fade to BLACKOUT, *then up to full for Finale*

EFFECTS PLOT

ACT I

Cue 1   **Dame:** "...more horseplay to it."   (Page 15)
       Knocking at door, off

Cue 2   **Wizard** winds clock   (Page 18)
       Clock ticks

Cue 3   **David:** "Stop the Clock. Stop it"   (Page 22)
       Clock strikes one: clap of thunder

Cue 4   **Mouse** climbs Clock   (Page 24)
       Clock strikes one

ACT II

Cue 5   At end of **Pixies'** dance   (Page 31)
       Trumpet sounds

Cue 6   **Dame:** "It certainly is quiet."   (Page 40)
       Loud bump, off

MADE AND PRINTED IN GREAT BRITAIN BY
LATIMER TREND AND CO LTD PLYMOUTH

MADE IN ENGLAND